Y0-CUQ-432

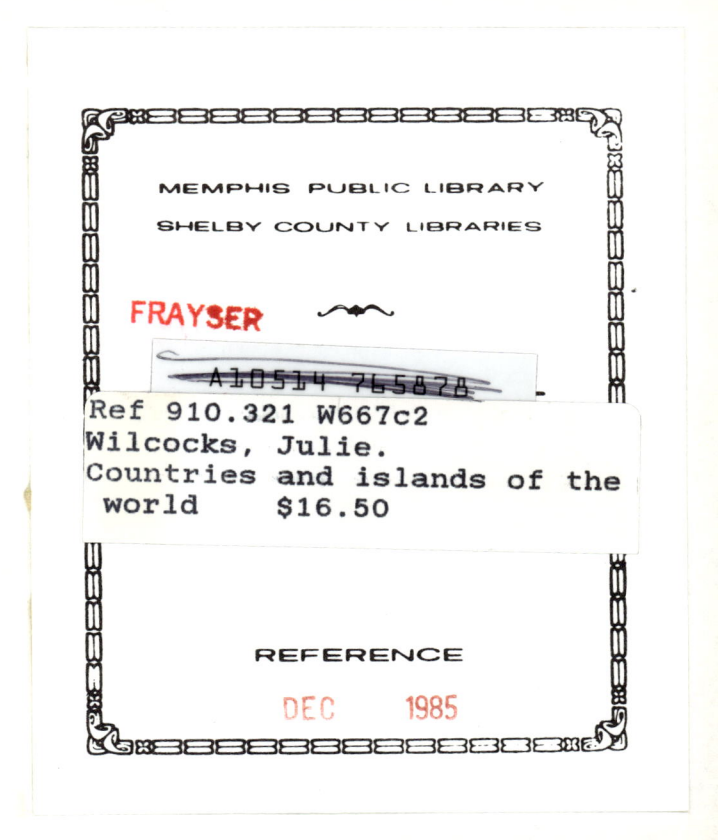

A10514 765878

MEMPHIS PUBLIC LIBRARY

SHELBY COUNTY LIBRARIES

FRAYSER

A10514 765878

Ref 910.321 W667c2
Wilcocks, Julie.
Countries and islands of the world $16.50

REFERENCE

DEC   1985

DISCARDED BY
MEMPHIS PUBLIC LIBRARY

COUNTRIES AND ISLANDS OF THE WORLD

COUNTRIES AND ISLANDS OF THE WORLD

a guide to nomenclature

SECOND EDITION

JULIE WILCOCKS
*University of the Witwatersrand
South Africa*

CLIVE BINGLEY　　LONDON

© 1985 Julie Wilcocks. Published by Clive Bingley Ltd, 7 Ridgmount Street, London WC1 and printed in Great Britain for the publishers by Redwood Burn Ltd, Trowbridge, Wiltshire. Typeset by Allset in 10 on 10 point Journal Roman. All rights reserved. No part of this publication may be photocopied, recorded or otherwise reproduced, stored in a retrieval system or transmitted in any form or by any electronic means without the prior permission of the publisher.

First edition published 1981
This revised edition published 1985

British Library Cataloguing in Publication Data

Wilcocks, Julie
   Countries and islands of the world.—2nd ed.
   1. Gazetteers
   I. Title
   910'.3'21   G103.5

ISBN 0 85157 383 5

Introduction to the first edition

Countries and islands of the world is intended as a reference guide to the many changes in name and government that have occurred in states all over the world in modern historical times. Dates of independence or of incorporation into federations have been included.

The arrangement is in alphabetical order and covers many states within federations as well as all fully independent nations.

The choice of entries apart from islands and fully independent countries has to be a selective one. All states and provinces within the major federations have been included (ie the USA, USSR, Australia, Canada and India) whether or not these subsidiary states have at one time been independent territories. Also included are those constituent states which are a key part of smaller federations (ie the United Arab Emirates and the Federation of Malaysia). In addition there are former kingdoms and principalities which have particularly featured in modern history (eg those which now make up Yugoslavia and Rumania).

The full name (or names) of each country has been included as a cross-reference. Where a country has more than one language in common use the main language versions are listed. As can be appreciated, 'official' names are usually a matter of choice. Arabic names have been transliterated as the embassies of their governments have stipulated. Areas appearing in italics are referred to elsewhere in alphabetical sequence.

Abbreviations frequently used are as follows:

USA   United States of America
USSR   Union of Soviet Socialist Republics
UK   United Kingdom of Great Britain and Northern Ireland
UN   The United Nations
UAR   United Arab Republic

The term 'part of' indicates that the country or island referred to is administered by another.

This work has been compiled primarily for the use of librarians at reference desks. A quick check can be made of former names, alternative names and current names of countries and islands, as well as some of the historical events connected with these changes in name and administration. I hope that Geography and History Departments at all levels of education will find it a handy reference work.

I acknowledge the valuable editing and expanding of the book in London by Rosamund McDougall.

                             Julie Wilcocks
                             University of the Witwatersrand
                             South Africa
                             1980

Introduction to the second edition

In updating this work on the countries and islands of the world, those islands which have changed their name recently have been included. In consequence more islands and island groups have been included. Where there has been further development of independence these facts have been updated.

The meaning of the term 'name' throughout the book is used in the widest sense, in that to distinguish between a spelling, a translation, an alternative name or a different language is beyond the scope of the work. What it is intended to show is that there are these various forms of name in the current writings of our time. The choice of entries again must be selective to keep the book at a level useful to small libraries, especially in schools, as a handy home reference for those who wish to follow current events on the map as it were, or for the philatelists and geographers.

Julie Wilcocks
University of the Witwatersrand
South Africa
1984

Bibliography

Atlases and gazetteers
The atlas of Africa, Jeune Afrique, 1973.
The Columbia Lippincott gazetteer of the world, Columbia University Press, 1961.
The international atlas, Philip, 1969.
The international geographic encyclopedia and atlas, Macmillan Press, 1979.
The Times atlas of the world, Times Books/J Bartholomew Ltd, 1980.

Journals
Geographic digest, ed H Fullard, Philip, 1963–83.

Other reference works
The American colonies, R C Simmons, Longman, 1976.
Geography of the USSR, J P Cole, Pelican Books, 1967.
Malaysia, J M Gullick, Benn, 1969.
News/Check's key to Africa, R Briggs, Checkpress, 1968.
Penguin dictionary of modern history, A W Palmer, Penguin Books, 1978.
Penguin encyclopedia of places, W G Moore, Penguin Books, 1978.
Place names of the world, A Room, David and Charles, 1974.
Statesman's yearbook, Macmillan, 1975–80 editions.
Whitaker's almanack, J Whitaker & Sons Ltd, 1960–84 editions.
The Europa yearbook, A world survey, Europa, vol 1 and vol 2, 1983.
Webster's new geographical dictionary, Merriam, 1980.
The new encyclopaedia Britannica, Micropaedia and Macropaedia, Benton, 1980.
Africa south of the Sahara, 1980–81, Europa, 1980.

A

AALAND (Island): alternative name for *Ahvenanmaa*, part of *Finland*.

ABACO (Island): alternative name for *Great Abaco*, part of *Bahamas*.

ABARIRINGA (Island): former name is *Canton* Island, one of the *Phoenix Islands*, part of *Kiribati*.

ABU DHABI: one of the seven component states of the *United Arab Emirates*. The sheikdom became a British protectorate in 1892 and joined the UAE in 1971.

ABYSSINIA: former name of *Ethiopia*.

ACHILL (Island): off the west coast of County Mayo, *Irish Republic*. Connected to the mainland by a bridge. Part of *Irish Republic*.

A C P STATES: see *African, Caribbean and Pacific States*.

ACTAEON GROUP: coral island group in the *Tuamotu Islands*. Discovered in 1606 by Queiros, part of *French Polynesia*.

ADELAIDE (Island): part of *Antarctica*, off the Antarctic peninsula.

ADEN COLONY: was a British crown colony in 1935, the surrounding region became *Aden Protectorate* in 1937, which became the independent People's Republic of Southern Yemen (or commonly *South Yemen*) on 30 November 1967, and *Peoples Democratic Republic of Yemen* on 30 November 1970.

ADEN PROTECTORATE: former name of part of *South Yemen*, name Aden Protectorate ceased use on independence in 1967.

ADMIRALTY (Island): in the *Alexander Archipelago*, part of the *USA*.

ADMIRALTY (Islands): alternative name for *Manus* Islands, in the *Bismarck Archipelago*, part of *Papua New Guinea*.

AFARS AND ISSAS: former name of *Djibouti*, name Afars and Issas in use from 1967 to 1977.

AFGHANISTAN: after the Afghan wars, an Anglo-Russian agreement was signed in 1907 which gave independence to Afghanistan under British influence. The British influence ended in 1919 and an independent kingdom continued until 1973, when the constitutional monarchy was replaced by government by presidential decree. Full name is *Democratic Republic of Afghanistan*.

AFOGNAK (Island): part of *USA*, off the coast of Alaska.

AFRICAN, CARIBBEAN AND PACIFIC STATES: known as the A C P States. On 1 January, 1981 a new five-year Lomé convention, known as Lomé II, was officially started. The agreement is between the

European Economic Community and these developing countries. As at September 1983 the countries involved are:

Antigua and Barbuda	Malawi
Bahamas	Mali
Barbados	Mauritania
Belize	Mauritius
Benin	Niger
Botswana	Nigeria
Burundi	Papua New Guinea
Cameroon	Rwanda
Cape Verde	Saint Lucia
Central African Republic	Saint Vincent and
Chad	the Grenadines
Comoros	São Tomé and Príncipe
Congo	Senegal
Djibouti	Seychelles
Dominica	Sierra Leone
Equatorial Guinea	Solomon Islands
Ethiopia	Somalia
Fiji	Sudan
Gabon	Suriname
Gambia	Swaziland
Ghana	Tanzania
Grenada	Togo
Guinea	Tonga
Guinea-Bissau	Trinidad and Tobago
Guyana	Tuvalu
Ivory Coast	Uganda
Jamaica	Upper Volta
Kenya	Vanuatu
Kiribati	Western Samoa
Lesotho	Zaire
Liberia	Zambia
Madagascar	Zimbabwe

AGALEGA (Island): one of the *Mascarene Islands,* part of *Mauritius.*

AHVENANMAA (Island): alternative names are *Aaland* and *Aland*, part of *Finland.*

AJMAN: one of the seven states of the *United Arab Emirates*. The skeikdom was formerly a British protectorate, joining the UAE in 1971.

AKIMISKI (Island): part of *Canada*, (Northwest Territory).

ALABAMA: the 22nd state to join the federal republic of the *USA*, it was set up as the Territory of Alabama in 1817 and achieved statehood in 1819.

ALAND (Island): alternative name for *Ahvenanmaa*, part of *Finland*.

ALASKA: originally discovered by Russian explorers, Alaska was sold to the *USA* in 1867. It became a US territory in 1912 but was not admitted as a state until 1959, when it became the 49th to join the federation.

ALBANIA: alternative name is Shqiperi, one of the *Balkan States*, which was under Ottoman rule from 1478 to 1912 when independence was proclaimed. Held by many nations in World War I, Italy occupied Albania in World War II, after which a socialist regime was set up. Full name is *Republika Popullore Socialiste e Shqiperërisë*.

ALBEMARLE (Island): alternative name for *Isabela*, island in the *Galapagos Islands*, part of *Ecuador*.

ALBERTA: one of the twelve constituent provinces of *Canada*, Alberta was sold to the confederation in 1882 by the Hudson's Bay Company. Alberta became a province in 1905.

ALDABRA (Island): one of the *Seychelles* group.

ALEUTIAN ISLANDS: composed of *Fox Islands, Andreanof Islands, Rat Islands, Near Islands* plus many individual islands, part of the *USA*.

ALEXANDER (Island): part of *Antarctica*, off the Antarctic peninsula.

ALEXANDER ARCHIPELAGO: composed of *Chichagof, Baranof, Admiralty, Kupreanof, Kuiu, Prince of Wales* and *Revillagigedo* islands as well as minor islands of Mitkof, Wrangell and other uninhabited islands, part of *USA*.

ALGERIA: France occupied Algeria in 1830 and independence was gained 3 July 1962. Full names are: *El Djemhouria El Djazaïria* or *République Algérienne Démocratique et Populaire*.

AL-JAMAHIRIYAH AL-ARABIYA AL-LIBYA AL-SHABIYA AL-ISHTIRAKIYA: see *Libya*.

AL-JOUMHOURIYAT AL-LOUBNANIAT: see *Lebanon*.

AL-JUMHOURIYA AL-ARABIA AL-YAMANIA: see *Yemen Arab Republic*.

AL-JUMHOURIYA AL-ARABIYA AS-SOURIYA: see *Syria*.

AL-JUMHOURIYA AL-IRAQIA: see *Iraq*.

AL-JUMHOURIYA ATTUNISIA: see *Tunisia*.

AL-MAMLAKA AL-'ARABIYA AS-SA'UDIYA: see *Saudi Arabia*.

AL-MAMLAKA AL-MAGHREBIA: see *Morocco*.

AL-MAMLAKA AL-URDUNIYA AL-HASHEMIYAH: see *Jordan*.

ALOR (Island): alternative name is *Ombai*, island in the *Lesser Sunda Islands,* part of *Indonesia.*

AMAMI-GUNTO (Island): a group in the *Ryukyu Islands*, composed of *Amami-Oshima* Island and several smaller islands, part of *Japan.*

AMAMI-OSHIMA (Island): one of the *Amami-Gunto* group in the *Ryukyu Islands*, part of *Japan.*

AMBOINA (Island): in the *Moluccas Group*, part of *Indonesia.*

AMERICAN SAMOA: alternative name is *Eastern Samoa.* The *Samoa Islands* were discovered by the Dutch in 1722, belonged to Germany from 1899 to 1914, and were mandated to New Zealand from 1920 to 1947. In 1947 the UN split the islands, whereby the Territory of *Western Samoa* fell under trusteeship to New Zealand and the rest of the islands, known as American Samoa belong to the *USA.* Composed of *Tutuila*, Aunuu, Manua Group, Swains and Rose.

AMUND RINGNES (Island): one of the *Queen Elizabeth Islands*, part of *Canada.*

ANDAMAN ISLANDS: composed of *North Andaman, Middle Andaman,* Baratang, *South Andaman,* Rutland and smaller islands, part of *India.*

ANDAMAN AND NICOBAR ISLANDS: one of the nine union territories of *India*; composed of the *Andaman* Islands and the *Nicobar* Islands.

ANDHRA PRADESH: one of the twenty-one states of *India,* it came into being in 1953 on the partition of India, taking in parts of the former presidency of Madras and the princely state of Hyderabad.

ANDORRA: a semi-independent principality under the suzerainty of France and Spain to which countries a nominal tribute is paid. Full name in the official Catalan language is *Principat d'Andorra* (formerly Lés Vallées d'Andorra or Valls d'Andorra).

ANDREANOF ISLANDS: included in the *Aleutian Islands.* Composed of Amlia, Atka, Adak, Kanaga, Tanaga and other small islands, part of *USA.*

ANDROS (Island): one of the *Cyclades Islands,* part of *Greece.*

ANDROS (Islands): several unnamed islands, part of the *Bahamas.*

ANGEL DE LA GUARDA (Island): part of *Mexico.*

ANGLESEY (Island): in the Irish Sea off the northwest coast of *Wales.* The island is a Welsh county, part of *UK.*

ANGLO-EGYPTIAN SUDAN: former name of *Sudan*. Name Anglo-Egyptian Sudan used from 1899 to 1956.

ANGOLA: includes the exclave of *Cabinda*. Angola was a Portuguese colony from 1575 to 1951 when it became an Overseas Province. Independence was gained on 11 November 1975.

ANGUILLA (Island): former name is *Snake Island*, island is in the *Leeward Islands* of the *Lesser Antilles* in the *West Indies*. St Kitts—Nevis—Anguilla formed part of the West Indies Associated States in 1967 in association with Britain; each state having internal self-government. On 19 December 1980 Anguilla was formally separated from this associated state and became a separate dependent territory of the *UK*.

ANJOUAN (Island): part of the *Comoro Islands*.

ANNAM: former name of part of *Vietnam*.

ANNOBÓN (Isla de): the island was formally called Annobon, then the name was changed to *Pagalu* and has been renamed Annobón, part of *Equatorial Guinea*.

ANTARCTICA: various sections are claimed by the following countries: *Queen Maud Land* (*Norway*); *Australian Antarctic Territory*, *French Southern and Antarctic Lands*, *Ross Dependency* (*New Zealand*); other claims by *USA, Chile, Argentina, UK* and *USSR*. Islands belonging to the continent of Antarctica are: *Adelaide Island* (*UK*), *Alexander Island* (*UK*), *Berkner Island* (*Argentina*), *Charcot Island* (*UK*), *Kerguelen Archipelago* (*France*).

ANTICOSTI (Island): part of *Canada*.

ANTIGUA AND BARBUDA (Islands): in the *Leeward Islands* of the *Lesser Antilles* in the *West Indies*. Colonial rule ended on 27 February 1967 when the islands became a state in association with Britain. Included in the State is the island of *Redonda*. Antigua was first settled by the English in 1632. Full independence was gained on 1 November 1981.

ANTILLES: comprise *Greater Antilles* and *Lesser Antilles* in the *West Indies*.

ANTIPODES (Islands): an outlying island group southeast of South Island, New Zealand, part of *New Zealand*.

AOMEN: former name of *Macao*.

ARABIA: former name of *Saudi Arabia*. Name changed in 1932.

ARAB REPUBLIC OF EGYPT: see *Egypt*.

ARAN (Island): in the Atlantic Ocean off the west coast of County Donegal, *Irish Republic*, of which it is a part.

ARAN ISLANDS: group of islands off the coast of County Galway, Irish Republic. Inishmore is the largest island; others are Inishmaan and Inisheer. Part of *Irish Republic*.

ARCHIPELAGO DE COLON: alternative name for the *Galapagos Islands*, alternatively the *Colon Islands*, part of *Ecuador*.

ARGENTINA: formerly a Spanish viceroyalty of Argentina, *Uruguay*, *Paraguay* and *Bolivia*. Viceroy deposed on 25 May 1810; independence proclaimed on 9 July 1816. Part of *Tierra del Fuego* is governed by Argentina. Full name is *República Argentina*.

ARIZONA: the area became part of the US Territory of *New Mexico* in 1850 and was organized as a separate territory in 1863. It became a fully federated state of the *USA* in 1912, the 48th to join the Union.

ARKANSAS: Arkansas, the 25th state to join the *USA*, began as part of the Territory of *Missouri* in 1812. It became a separate territory in 1819 and a state of the Union in 1836.

ARMENIAN SOVIET SOCIALIST REPUBLIC: one of the fifteen constituent republics of the *USSR*. It was acquired by *Russia* from *Persia* in 1828 and became independent after the 1917 Bolshevik revolution. In 1922 it joined *Georgia* and *Azerbaijan* to form the Transcaucasian SFSR, but in 1936 became a separate republic. The term 'Armenia' is also used to cover the former region and kingdom of Asia Minor, comprising parts of present-day Armenia, northeast *Turkey* and Iranian *Azerbaijan*.

ARRAN (Island): part of *Scotland, UK*.

ARU ISLANDS: composed of Kola, Wokam, Kobrot, Maikoor, *Trangan* islands which are in the *Moluccas Group*, part of *Indonesia*.

ARUBA (Island): part of the *Netherlands Antilles*.

ARUNACHAL PRADESH: one of the nine union territories of *India* since 1972, it was known as the North-East Frontier Agency Special Territory until 1947, when it became part of *Assam*.

ASCENSION (Island): part of *St Helena* island.

ASINARA (Island): one of the islands off the coast of *Sardinia*, part of *Italy*.

ASSAM: one of the twenty-one states of *India*, it was before the partition of India in 1947 one of its larger provinces. Assam lost territory to the newly created states of *Nagaland* (1961), *Manipur* (1972), *Meghalaya* (1972), and *Tripura* (1972). The union territory of *Mizoram* was also created from within Assam in 1972, reducing its boundaries to their present extent.

AUCKLAND (Islands): an outlying island group south of South Island, New Zealand. Part of *New Zealand*.

AUSTRALASIA: large area of the South Pacific including Australia, New Zealand, New Guinea, and adjacent islands. The term tends to be flexible and sometimes refers to the whole of *Oceania*.

AUSTRALIA: full name is Commonwealth of Australia. Cook landed in 1770 and claimed the coast for Great Britain, where a Penal Colony was established in 1788. A crown colony of *Victoria* was formed in 1824 and gold was struck in 1851, Victoria then separated from *New South Wales*. In 1901 the colonies of New South Wales, Victoria, *Queensland, South Australia, Western Australia* and *Tasmania* were federated into a Commonwealth. *Northern Territory* joined the federation in 1911; Canberra (*Australian Capital Territory*) was built in the same year. Islands included in Australia are: *Bathurst, Furneaux Group, Groot Eylandt, Kangaroo, Cocos,* Ashmore, Cartier, Coral Sea Islands, Heard, McDonald, *Norfolk, King, Melville Islands, Christmas, Moreton* and *Stradbroke*.

AUSTRALIAN ANTARCTIC TERRITORY: see *Antarctica*.

AUSTRALIAN CAPITAL TERRITORY: one of the two territories which make up the constituent states and territories of *Australia*, it is an enclave within *New South Wales*. Until 1938 it was known as the Federal Capital Territory. Much of the area was ceded to the Commonwealth of Australia by New South Wales in 1911, the remainder being handed over in 1915.

AUSTRIA: full name is *Republik Österreich*. An Austro-Hungarian monarchy was established in 1867 and collapsed in 1918 when German Austria proclaimed a Republic. In 1940 Austria was incorporated into *Germany* and captured by Soviet and US troops in 1945. In 1946 Austria was formally recognized as an independent state by Western powers and a peace treaty was signed in 1955.

AVAL: former name of *Bahrein*.

AWAL: former name of *Bahrein*.

AXEL HEIBERG (Island): one of the *Queen Elizabeth Islands*, part of *Canada*.

AZAD KASHMIRI: see *Kashmir*.

AZERBAIJAN SOVIET SOCIALIST REPUBLIC: or Azerbaidzhan. One of the fifteen constituent republics of the *USSR*. *Russia* acquired the territory from *Persia* in the 19th century. Soon after the 1917 revolution Azerbaijan joined *Armenian SSR* and *Georgian SSR* to form the Transcaucasian SFSR. In 1936 it became a separate republic.

AZORES ISLANDS: composed of *São Miguel, Pico, Terceira, Faial, São Jorge,* Graciosa and Flores islands, part of *Portugal.*

B

BABELTHUAP (Island): one of the *Palau Islands*, which is in the *Caroline Islands*, part of the *Pacific Islands (USA)*.

BACAN (Island): one of the *Moluccas Group*, part of *Indonesia*.

BAFFIN (Island): part of *Canada*, north of Hudson Bay.

BAHAMAS: early in the 17th century the British arrived on the Bahamas. The first Royal Governor was appointed in 1717. The islands were surrendered to the Spanish in 1781 but retaken by the British in 1783. They gained their independence on 10 July 1973. The main islands they comprise are *Abaco, Andros, Cat, Eleuthera, Grand Bahama, Inagua, Long, New Providence, San Salvador* islands. Full name is *Commonwealth of the Bahamas*.

BAHRAIN (Island): alternative name for *Bahrein*.

BAHRAYN (Island): alternative name for *Bahrein*.

BAHREIN (Island): former names are *Aval* and *Awal*, alternative names are *Bahrein* and *Bahrayn*. Bahrein was occupied by the Portuguese in 1507. The Persian Arabs were rulers from 1602 and the present family have ruled from 1783 as an independent Arab sheikdom. From 1861 there has been British protection.

BALEARIC ISLANDS: composed of *Majorca, Ibiza, Minorca, Formentera* plus smaller islands; part of *Spain*.

BALI (Island): one of the *Lesser Sunda Islands*, part of *Indonesia*.

BALKAN STATES: refers to the southeast European countries which were once under the complete control of the *Ottoman Empire*, ie *Bulgaria, Rumania, Albania* and *Yugoslavia*.

BANABA (Island): former name is *Ocean* Island, part of *Kiribati*.

BANANAL (Island): part of *Brazil*.

BANDA ORIENTAL: former name of *Uruguay*. Known as Banda Oriental from 16th century until about 1827.

BANGGAI ARCHIPELAGO: includes *Peleng* and Banggai Islands, part of *Indonesia*.

BANGKA (Island): part of *Indonesia*.

BANGLADESH: former name was *East Pakistan*. The British occupied *India* and *Pakistan*; authority was handed over on 15 August 1947. East Pakistan split from *West Pakistan* to become the *People's Republic of Bangladesh* on 22 December 1971. *Dakhin Shabazpur* island is included in Bangladesh.

BANKS (Island): part of *Canada*, (British Columbia).

BANKS (Islands): part of *Canada*, (Northwest Territory).

BARANOF (Island): in the *Alexander Archipelago*, part of *USA*.

BARBADOS (Island): was first settled by the British in 1627 and was a Crown Colony from 1652. Barbados became independent on 30 November 1966. Barbados lies in the *Lesser Antilles*.

BARBUDA (Island): see *Antigua and Barbuda* (Islands).

BARDSEY (Island): in the Irish Sea off the coast of Caernarvonshire, *Wales*; part of *UK*.

BARRA (Island): one of the *Outer Hebrides*, off the coast of *Scotland*, part of the *UK*.

BASILAN (Island): part of the *Philippines*.

BASSE-TERRE (Island): part of *Guadeloupe*.

BASUTOLAND: former name of *Lesotho*, name changed on 4 October 1966.

BATHURST (Island): part of *Australia*.

BATHURST (Island): one of the *Parry Islands*, part of *Canada*.

BECHUANALAND PROTECTORATE: former name of *Botswana*, the name Bechuanaland was used from 1885 until 30 September 1966.

BELAU (Islands): full name is the *Republic of Belau*, former name is the *Palau Islands*. Composed of *Babelthuap*, Arakabesan, Koror and Malakal. Under the Spanish regime they were administered by the Caroline Islands and sold to Germany in 1899. They were seized in 1914 and mandated to Japan in 1919. After World War II they became part of *Pacific Islands (USA)*. Gained independence on 1 January 1981.

BELGIAN CONGO: former name of *Zaïre*, the name Belgian Congo was used from 28 November 1908 to 30 June 1960. Name Zaïre was used from 27 October 1971. Between 30 June 1960 and 27 October 1971 the country was known as *Congo-Kinshasa*.

BELGIUM: in the 15th century the area was under a Duchy of Burgundy. In 1797 Belgium went from Austrian jurisdiction to that of *France*. In 1815 the *Netherlands* took over from France. In 1830 a Belgian independent king was appointed and the monarchy remains. Belgium was overrun by Germany during both wars but the monarchy re-established itself. Full names are *Royaume de Belgique* and *Koninkrijk België*.

BELITUNG (Island): alternative name of *Billiton*, part of *Indonesia*.

BELIZE: in the mid 17th century the British claimed Belize from *Guatemala*. Renaming it *British Honduras*, the country was a Jamaican dependency from 1882 to 1884, after which it became an independent colony under Britain. Self-government was attained in 1964. The name changed back to Belize on 1 June 1973, and full independence was achieved on 21 October 1981.

BELORUSSIAN SOVIET SOCIALIST REPUBLIC: also known formerly as White Russia, it is one of the fifteen constituent republics of the *USSR*. Through the Polish partitions of the 18th century, the whole area of Belorussia passed to *Russia*. In 1921 the Treaty of Riga awarded western Belorussia to *Poland*. The eastern part formed the Belorussian SSR, which joined the USSR in 1922. The republic has its own seat at the UN.

BENIN: former name is *Dahomey*, the name Benin has been in use since 1975. The area was part of *French West Africa* from 1904 to 1958, the Republic of Dahomey was proclaimed in 1958 and independence gained on 1 August 1960. Full name is *République Populaire du Benin* or *People's Republic of Benin*.

BERING (Island): part of the *USSR*.

BERKNER (Island): part of *Antarctica*, claimed by the *UK*.

BERMUDA (Islands): the group has been a British crown colony since 1684, and has been internally self-governed since 8 June 1968. A former name was *Somers Islands*.

BHARAT: alternative name of *India*.

BHUTAN: alternative name is *Druk-yul*. Bhutan as a protectorate of *India* fell under British rule from 1866 to 1947. With the independence of India, foreign affairs are now conducted by India instead of Britain. Independence, apart from foreign affairs, has been enjoyed since 1910.

BIAFRA: former name of part of *Nigeria*. The secession of the independent Republic of Biafra from Nigeria was on 30 May 1967. The secession ended in January 1970.

BIAK (Island): is included in *West Irian*, part of *Indonesia*.

BIHAR: one of the twenty-one states of *India*, it is a seat of Buddhism. Occupied by Moslems in 1193, the Delhi Sultans in 1497 and the British in 1765, who merged it with Bengal. In 1912 the province of Bihar and Orissa was set up and in 1936 Bihar became a separate province. An eastern section was transferred to West Bengal in 1956.

BILLITON (Island): alternative name is *Belitung*, part of *Indonesia*.

BINTAN (Island): part of *Indonesia*.

BIOKO (Island): former names are Fernando Póo until 1973, followed by Macias Nguema Biyogo, part of *Equatorial Guinea*.

BIRMAH: former name of *Burma*.

BISAYAS: alternative name for *Visayan Islands*.

BISMARCK ARCHIPELAGO: composed of *New Britain, New Ireland, Lavongai, Admiralty* and smaller islands; part of *Papua New Guinea*.

BLASKET ISLANDS: group of islands off the coast of County Kerry, part of the *Irish Republic*.

BOA VISTA (Island): part of *Cape Verde Islands*.

BOBIAN (Island): alternative name for *Bubiyan* Island, part of *Kuwait*.

BOETOENG (Island): former name of *Butung* Island, part of *Indonesia*.

BOHEMIA: a kingdom since the Middle Ages which reached its height of power within the Holy Roman Empire in the 14th century, it was reduced to a Hapsburg crown land in 1627 and after subsequent domination by Austria-Hungary it reached full independence again only after World War I. In 1918 Bohemia became the central part of the new state of *Czechoslovakia*.

BOHOL (Island): one of the *Visayan Islands*, part of the *Philippines*.

BOLIVIA: in 1559 the area was part of Upper Peru and attached to the viceroyalty of *Peru*. In 1776 it was transferred to the viceroyalty of La Plata until 1824. In 1825 the formation of a republic occurred and the area became independent as Bolivia. Full name *Républica de Bolivia*.

BOLSHEVIK (Island): one of the *Severnaya Zemlya Islands*, part of the *USSR*.

BOLSHOY LYAKHOVSKIY (Island): under *Lyakhovskiy Island*, part of the *USSR*.

BOLSHOY SHANTAR (Island): part of *USSR*.

BONAIRE (Island): part of *Netherlands Antilles*.

BONIN (Islands): alternative name is *Ogasawara-Gunto* (Islands). Were handed back to Japan by USA on 26 June 1968, part of *Japan*.

BOPHUTHATSWANA: independent homeland from 6 December 1977, under *South Africa*.

BORDEN (Island): part of *Canada*, (Northwest Territory).

BORNEO (Island): composed of four parts to the one island: *Kalimantan*, part of *Indonesia*; *Sarawak*, part of *Malaysia*; *Brunei*, (independent sultanate) and *Sabah*, part of *Malaysia*.

BORNHOLM (Island): part of *Denmark*.

BOSNIA AND HERCOGOVINA: one of the six constituent republics of *Yugoslavia* since 1945, the two provinces lay under Turkish influence until in 1878 Austria-Hungary took over their administration. The formal annexation of Bosnia and Hercogovina by *Austria* in 1908 brought about the Bosnian crisis which precipitated World War I. Between the wars they formed part of the Kingdom of Yugoslavia; during World War II they became part of the German puppet state of *Croatia*.

BOTSWANA: former name was *Bechuanaland Protectorate*, from 1885-1966 British Bechuanaland was the region of the northern Cape lying south of the Molopo River, Bechuanaland Protectorate was the area north of the Molopo River. British Bechuanaland was attached to the Cape of Good Hope in 1895 and became part of the Union of South Africa in 1910. The northern part remained a Protectorate until the independence of Botswana on 30 September 1966.

BOUGAINVILLE (Island): part of *Papua New Guinea*, originally part of the *Solomon Islands*.

BOUNTY (Islands): outlying islands off the coast of New Zealand discovered by Captain Bligh of the HMS Bounty in 1788. Part of *New Zealand*.

BOURBON (Island): former name of *Réunion*.

BOUVET (Island): in the South Atlantic, discovered by the French in 1739 but claimed in 1927 by Norway. Placed under Norwegian sovereignty in 1928 and made a dependency of *Norway* in 1930.

BRAC (Island): former name is *Brazza Island*, part of *Yugoslavia*.

BRAVA (Island): part of the *Cape Verde Islands*.

BRAZIL: the Portuguese occupied the area from 1808 to 1889. They were then overthrown and a republic was established in 1889 called the United States of Brazil. Full name is now *República Federativa do Brasil*. Various islands controlled by Brazil are: *Bananal, Caviana, Gurupa, Marajo, Mexiana,* and *São Luis Islands*.

BRAZZA (Island): former name of *Brac Island*, part of *Yugoslavia*.

BRESSAY (Island): one of the *Shetland Islands*, in *Scotland*, part of the *UK*.

BRITAIN: or *Great Britain*; part of the *UK*, comprising *England, Wales* and *Scotland*.

BRITISH ANTARCTIC TERRITORY: includes all islands south of 60°South and between 20° and 80° West. Part of the *Falkland Island*

Dependencies became separate from the *Falkland Islands* under a High Commissioner on 3 March 1962, and were called British Antarctic Territory. This includes the British sector of *Antarctica*, Graham Land, *South Shetland, South Orkney*, and *Adelaide*.

BRITISH CAMEROON: former name of part of *Cameroon* and part of *Nigeria*, name changed on 1 October 1961.

BRITISH COLUMBIA: one of the twelve constituent provinces of *Canada*, British Columbia was under the influence of Britain until the Hudson's Bay Company acquired it in 1821. *Vancouver Island* became a British crown colony in 1849. In 1858 the new mainland colony of British Columbia was created. A reunited British Columbia and Vancouver joined the new confederation of Canada in 1871.

BRITISH EAST AFRICA: former name for *Kenya, Tanganyika, Uganda* and *Zanzibar*, the name was in use from 1919 until each area became independent.

BRITISH GUIANA: former name of *Guyana*, name changed on 26 May 1966.

BRITISH HONDURAS: former name of *Belize*. the area was known as Belize before 1882, and again after 1 June 1973.

BRITISH INDIAN OCEAN TERRITORY: this new colony was established in November 1965, comprising Farquhar, Desroches, *Aldabra* Islands and *Chagos Archipelago*. Farquhar, Desroches and *Aldabra* went to the *Seychelles* on their independence on 29 June 1976.

BRITISH MALAYA: former name of peninsular *Malaya*, now peninsular *Malaysia*.

BRITISH NORTH BORNEO: former name of *Sabah*, part of *Malaysia*, name changed on 16 September 1963.

BRITISH SOLOMON ISLANDS: former name of the *Solomon Islands*, the name changed on the 22 June 1975 and the Islands gained their independence on 7 July 1978.

BRITISH SOMALILAND: former name of part of *Somalia*, name changed on 26 June 1960.

BRITISH TOGOLAND: former name of part of *Ghana*. The area joined the *Gold Coast* in 1956, to become independent *Ghana* on 6 March 1957.

BRITISH VIRGIN ISLANDS: a presidency within the Leeward Islands colony. A British possession since 1648. The *Leeward Islands* colony defederated in 1956, and the Virgin Islands colony was established. Composed of *Tortola*, Virgin Gorda, Jost van Ryke, Anegada and many uninhabited islands.

BRITISH WEST INDIES: see under *West Indies*.

BRUNEI: Islamic sultanate under British protection from 1888 to 1906; was then placed under the rule of a British Resident, which was abolished in 1969. In 1971 full self-government was achieved. At the beginning of 1984 the sultanate became independent. On the island of *Borneo*.

BUBIYAN (Island): alternative name is *Bobian Island*, part of *Kuwait*.

BUGANDA: a kingdom within the Ugandan Protectorate which dated from 1900. Part of independent *Uganda* from 6 October 1962.

BUGD NAIRAMDAH MONGOL ARD ULS: see *Mongolia*.

BUKA (Island): part of *Papua New Guinea*, originally part of *Solomon Islands*.

BULGARIA: in 1908 Bulgaria was proclaimed independent. During World War II Bulgaria passed from German to Russian influence, when a socialist regime was established. Full name *Narodna Republika Bulgaria*.

BUNDESREPUBLIK DEUTSCHLAND: see *Federal Republic of Germany*.

BURKINO FASO: present name (changed in 1984) of *Upper Volta* (q.v.)

BURMA: former name is *Birmah*. In 1862 Britain annexed Burma into *India* and in 1937 it was separated from India. On 4 January 1948 it gained its independence from Britain as the Union of Burma. *Ramree* island is part of Burma. Full name is *Pyidaungsu Socialist Thammada Myanma Naingngandaw*.

BURRA (Islands): there are two islands, east and west, which are part of the *Shetland Islands* in *Scotland*, part of *UK*.

BURU (Island): former name is Boeroe Island. Island included in the *Moluccas Group*, part of *Indonesia*.

BURUNDI: Former name is *Urundi*. *Rwanda* was joined to Burundi in 1899 as a German colony. They were mandated to Belgium from 1919 to 1946. In 1946 the area became a UN trust territory and on 2 July 1962 the area split into Burundi and Rwanda, each becoming independent. Burundi retained its monarchy but under great civil strife, and since 1966 it has been a republic.

BUTARITARI (Island): former name is *Makin*, or Pitt Island, part of *Kiribati*.

BUTE (Island): in the firth of Clyde off the coast of *Scotland*, part of *UK*.

BUTON: (Island): alternative name for *Butung*, part of *Indonesia*.

BUTUNG (Island): alternative name is *Buton*, former name is *Boetoeng*, part of *Indonesia*.

BYLOT (Island): part of *Canada*, (Northwest Territory).

C

CABINDA: an exclave of *Angola*. Alternative name is *Kabinda*.

CABO VERDE (Ilhas do): alternative name of *Cape Verde Islands*.

CALDY (Island): off the south coast of *Wales*, part of the County of *Pembroke*, part of *UK*.

CALIFORNIA: originally colonized by the Spanish and the Mexicans, the last Mexican governor was driven out in 1845, and *Mexico* formally ceded the area to the *USA* in 1848. California became, in 1850, the 31st state to join the Union.

CAMBODIA: former name of *Kampuchea*, in full *Democratic Kampuchea*.

CAMEROON: name in full is *République Unie du Cameroun*; former names are German *Kamerun*, *British Cameroon* and *French Cameroun*. The area was a German colony until 1884. In 1919 the area was split between British and French mandates, the West being British and the East being French. On 1 January 1960 French Cameroun became independent. On 1 October 1961 the northern part of British Cameroon joined *Nigeria* and the southern part joined the independent French Cameroun. The United Republic of Cameroon came into being on 2 June 1972.

CAMPBELL (Island): outlying Island off the coast of *New Zealand*. Discovered in 1810, part of New Zealand.

CANADA: the French Royal Government settled in the 16th century. In the 18th century the British ruled on the St Lawrence, and 1759 saw the fall of Quebec. 1763 saw the fall of Montreal and in that same year British rule was established. In 1867 a confederation with other provinces led to the formation of the Dominion of Canada. The ten federated provinces and two territories of Canada are: *Alberta, British Columbia, Manitoba, New Brunswick, Newfoundland and Labrador, Nova Scotia, Ontario, Prince Edward Island, Quebec, Saskatchewan, Yukon Territory* and *Northwest Territories*. Coastal islands which fall under Canada are: *Akimiski, Anticosti, Baffin, Banks* (NW), *Banks* (British Columbia), *Borden, Bylot, Cape Breton, Coats, Ellef Ringnes, Jesus, King, King William, Mackenzie King, Manitoulin, Mansel, Montreal, Orleans, Parry Islands, Pitt, Prince Charles, Prince of Wales, Princess Royal, Queen Charlotte Islands, Queen Elizabeth Islands, St Joseph, Stefansson, Somerset, Southampton, Vancouver, Victoria, Magdalen Islands*.

CANAL ZONE: alternative name of *Panama Canal Zone*.

CANARY ISLANDS: composed of *La Palma, Gomera, Hierro, Tenerife, Lanzarote, Fuerteventura, Grand Canary*, and smaller islands, part of *Spain*.

CANDIA (Island): former name of *Crete*, part of *Greece*.

CANNANORE ISLANDS: alternative name of *Laccadive Islands*, part of *India*.

CANTON (Island): former name of *Abariringa*, one of the *Phoenix Islands*, part of *Kiribati*.

CAPE BRETON (Island): part of *Canada*, (Nova Scotia).

CAPE COLONY: was a British Colony founded in 1795, with Dutch rule reestablished in 1803 and the British retaking control in 1806. Other crown colonies of Kaffraria and *Bechuanaland* were established and merged with the Cape Colony in 1865 and 1895 respectively. With the founding of the Union of *South Africa*, the Cape Colony became the *Cape of Good Hope* Province.

CAPE OF GOOD HOPE: province of *Republic of South Africa*. It was a British colony known as *Cape Colony* from 1795 to 1910, when it joined the *Union of South Africa*.

CAPE VERDE ISLANDS: Portuguese colony until independence on 5 July 1975. Islands form two groups, *Windward* and *Leeward*. Windward group comprises *Santo Antão, São Vicente, São Nicolan, Sal, Boa Vista*; Leeward group comprises *Maio, São Tiago, Fogo, Brava*, plus many smaller islands. Full name is *Républica de Cabo Verde*.

CAPRERA (Island): one of the Islands off the coast of *Sardinia* and connected by a causeway to *La Maddalena* Island, part of *Italy*.

CARIBEES (Islands): alternative name for *Lesser Antilles* in the *West Indies*.

CAROLINE ISLANDS: former name is *New Philippines*, composed of *Kusaie, Ponape, Belau, Truk, Yap*, and smaller islands. These Islands were annexed by Spain in 1686 and purchased by Germany in 1899 to be seized by Japan in 1914 and mandated to Japan in 1919. Placed under US trusteeship in 1947 as the *Pacific Islands (USA)*. The Republic of *Belau* gained independence on 1 January 1981.

CAT (Island): part of the *Bahamas*.

CATANDUANES (Island): part of the *Philippines*.

CAVIANA (Island): part of *Brazil*.

CAYMAN ISLANDS: a dependency of *Jamaica* until 1959, composed of *Grand Cayman*, Little Cayman, Cayman Brac. In 1670 Spain gave the islands to Britain and in July 1959 the islands became a self-governing dependent territory of the *UK*.

CEBU (Island): former name is *Zebu*, one of the *Visayan Islands*, part of the *Philippines*.

CELEBES (Island): alternative name is *Sulawesi*, island in the *Greater Sunda Islands*, part of *Indonesia*.

CENTRAL AFRICAN EMPIRE: former name (1977 to 1979) of *Central African Republic*.

CENTRAL AFRICAN REPUBLIC: former name is *Ubangi-Shari*, dating from about 1889. The area then became part of *French Equatorial Africa* in 1919. Independence was gained on 13 August 1960 and the area became the *Central African Empire* in December 1977. Alternative full name was *Empire Centrafricain*. Name reverted to Central African Republic on 21 September 1979.

CENTRAL AMERICAN FEDERATION: former name (1823 to 1838) of an area now comprising the five countries *El Salvador, Costa Rica, Honduras, Nicaragua, Guatemala*.

CEPHALONIA (Island): alternative name is *Kefallinia*, one of the *Ionian Islands*, part of *Greece*.

CERAM (Island): alternative name is *Seram*, or Serang, one of the *Moluccas Group*, part of *Indonesia*.

CERIGO (Island): former name of *Cythera*, part of *Greece*.

CESKOSLOVENSKA SOCIALISTICKA REPUBLIKA: see *Czechoslovakia*.

CEUTA: enclave in *Morocco*, belonging to *Spain*.

CEYLON (Island): former name of *Sri Lanka*, before that it was known as *Serendib*. Name changed to Sri Lanka on 22 May 1972.

CHAD: alternative name is *Tchad*. First penetration in the late 19th century by French. Occupied by 1913 as part of *French Equatorial Africa*. Became a separate colony from *Ubangi-Shari* in 1920. Became the Republic of Chad within French Community on 26 November 1958 and fully independent on 11 August 1960. Full name: *République du Tchad*.

CHAF ARINAS (Islands): alternative name is Zafarin Islands. Island group in the Mediterranean Sea near *Melilla*, part of *Spain*.

CHAGOS ARCHIPELAGO: part of the *British Indian Ocean Territory*.

CHANDIGARH: one of the nine union territories of *India* since 1966.

CHANNEL ISLANDS: former name is *Norman Isles*. These islands lie off the north-west coast of France and have belonged to the Crown of England since 1106. They have their own legal and administrative systems but the United Kingdom is responsible for defence and International Relations. Composed of *Jersey, Guernsey*, Alderney, *Sark*, Jethou, *Herm*, Brechou, and Lihou islands.

CHARCOT (Island): part of *Antarctica*, claimed by *UK*.

CHATHAM ISLANDS: group of islands in the Pacific Ocean, east of New Zealand. The two main islands are Chatham Island and *Pitt* Island, discovered in 1791, part of *New Zealand*.

CHATHAM (Island): alternative name for San Cristobal, one of the *Galapagos Islands*, part of *Ecuador*.

CHAVES (Island): alternative name for *Santa Cruz* one of the *Galapagos Islands*, part of *Ecuador*.

CHEJU (Island): former name is *Quelpart, Saishu*, part of *South Korea*.

CHERSO (Island): former name of *Cres*, part of *Yugoslavia*.

CHESTERFIELD (Islands): group in the Coral Sea off the coast of Queensland, Australia. Owned by *France*.

CHICHAGOF (Island): in the *Alexander Archipelago*, part of the *USA*.

CHILE: discovered by the Spanish in the 16th century and remained under Spanish rule until 1810. The area was part of the viceroyalty of *Peru*. Independence was gained in 1818. Islands administered by Chile are: *Chiloe, Easter, Magdalena, Riesco, Wellington, Juan Fernandez, Sala Y Gomez, San Felix, San Ambrosio, Guamblin, Chonos Archipelago, Reina Adelaida Archipelago, Madre de Dios Archipelago*, and part of *Tierra del Fuego*. Full name is *República de Chile*.

CHILOE (Island): north of the *Chonos Archipelago*, off the coast of southwest *Chile*, of which it is part.

CHINA: alternative name is *Mainland China*, name in Pinyin is *Zhongguo*. Various imperial dynasties ruled China for many centuries up to 1912 when the Republic of China was formed. By 1949 the Chinese Peoples' Republic had formed as a socialist regime and the Nationalists had taken refuge on the island of *Formosa*. The Japanese occupied *Manchuria* and established an independent state of *Manchukuo* from 1932 to 1949, when it was reclaimed for China. The island of *Hainan* is administered by China. Full names are *People's Republic of China* or *Chung-Hua Jen-Min Kung-Ho Kuo*.

CHIOS (Island): alternative name is *Khios*. Sometimes included in the *Sporadhes* Islands, part of *Greece*.

CHOISEUL (Island): part of the *Solomon Islands*.

CHONOS ARCHIPELAGO: group of islands off the coast of southwest *Chile*.

CHOSUN MINCHU-CHUI INMIN KONGHWA-GUK: see *North Korea*.

CHRISTMAS (Island): former name of *Kirimati* island, one of the *Line Islands*, part of *Kiribati*.

CHRISTMAS (Island): from 1900 until 1957 the island was part of the crown colony of *Singapore*. It was occupied by the Japanese from 1942 to 1945. Now under *Australia*, administered as her territory from 1 October 1958.

CHUNG-HUA JEN-MIN KUNG-HO KUO: see *China*.

CISKEI: an independent homeland created on 4 December 1981 in the Republic of *South Africa*.

CITTA DEL VATICANO: alternative name of *Vatican City*.

CLARENCE (Island): in *Tierro del Fuego*, part of *Chile*.

CLARION (Island): alternative name is Santa Rosa, one of the *Revilla Gigedo Islands* in the Pacific Ocean off the coast of Colima, part of *Mexico*.

CLEAR ISLE: off the coast of County Cork, *Irish Republic*, of which it is part.

COATS (Island): part of *Canada*, (Northwest Territory).

COCHIN CHINA: former name of *Vietnam*. The area was named Cochin China before 1945, Vietnam from 1945 to 1954 and from 1976 onwards, and *South Vietnam* from 1954 to 1976.

COCOS ISLANDS: alternative name is *Keeling Islands*. Discovered by Captain Keeling in 1609, it was a British possession from 1857, and administered by *Ceylon* from 1878. The settlement of *Singapore* controlled the islands from 1903 until *Australia* took over on 23 November 1955. Composed of West, Home and Direction islands and many small coral islands.

COIBA (Island): off the coast of Panama in the Pacific Ocean. Part of *Panama*.

COLOMBIA: the name is derived from Columbus, the discoveror of the New World. Colombia was included in the Spanish viceroyalty of *New Granada* in 1717 with modern *Panama, Venezuela* and *Ecuador*; Greater Colombia became independent in 1819. In 1822 the area of Ecuador formed part of Greater Colombia. In 1830 Colombia and Panama emerged as the Republic of New Granada. The United States of New Granada was formed in 1861 and then the United States of Colombia in 1863. Finally in 1885 the Republic of Colombia was formed. The Republic of Panama was formed in 1903 when Colombia's boundaries were settled. Full name is *République de Colombia*. Colombia administers the island of *Malpelo*.

COLON ISLANDS: alternative name for the *Galapagos Group*, part of *Ecuador*.

COLONSAY (Island): one of the *Inner Hebrides*, off the coast of *Scotland*, part of the *UK*.

COLORADO: under dispute between French and Spanish settlers until it was sold to the *USA* in the Louisana Purchase of 1803, Colorado eventually joined the Union in 1876 as its 38th member state.

COMMONWEALTH COUNTRIES: the Commonwealth is a free association of the 48 (in 1984) sovereign independent states listed below: *Antigua and Barbuda, Australia, Bahamas, Bangladesh, Barbados, Belize, Botswana, Canada, Cyprus, Dominica, Fiji, Gambia* (The), *Ghana, Great Britain, Grenada, Guyana, India, Jamaica, Kenya, Kiribati, Lesotho, Malawi, Malaysia, Malta, Maldives, Mauritius, Nauru, New Zealand, Nigeria, Papua New Guinea, Saint Kitts-Nevis, Saint Lucia, Saint Vincent and the Grenadines, Seychelles, Sierra Leone, Singapore, Solomon Islands, Sri Lanka, Swaziland, Tanzania, Tonga, Trinidad and Tobago, Tuvalu, Uganda, Vanuatu, Western Samoa, Zambia, Zimbabwe.*

COMMONWEALTH OF AUSTRALIA: see *Australia*.

COMMONWEALTH OF THE BAHAMAS: see *Bahamas*.

COMORO (Islands): came under French protection in 1886. In 1912 they became a French colony and in January 1947 a French overseas territory. Internal autonomy was achieved on 27 January 1962 and independence on 6 July 1975 for all islands except Mayotte which wished to remain under France. The official long form of the name has changed from the Republic of the Comoros to the Federal and Islamic Republic of the Comoros in 1979. The islands are composed of Grande Comore, *Anjouan, Mohéli, Mayotte* and small islands.

CON HOA XA HOI CHU NGHIA VIET NAM: see *Vietnam*.

CONGO: or *Peoples Republic of the Congo*; former name is *Middle Congo*, known under this name as part of *French Equatorial Africa* since 1910. The Republic of Congo was formed as a member state of the French Community on 28 November 1958 and independence gained on 15 August 1960. To distinguish itself from its southern neighbour (now *Zaïre*) it became known as *Congo-Brazzaville* from 1960 to 1971. The country's name changed to its full one of *République Populaire du Congo* in December 1969.

CONGO-BRAZZAVILLE: former name of *Congo*. Before 1958 it was *Middle Congo* and between 1960 and 1971 it was Congo-Brazzaville. Between 1958 and 1960 and after 1971 it was called *Congo*.

CONGO FREE STATE: former name of *Zaïre*. It was Congo Free State between 1885 and 1908 and became Zaïre on 27 October 1971.

CONGO-KINSHASA: former name of *Zaïre*. It was known as *Belgian Congo* before 1960, Congo-Kinshasa from 1960 to 1971 and Zaïre after 1971.

CONNECTICUT: the 5th state to join the federal republic of the *USA* (in 1788) Connecticut was one of the first regions to be formed into a colony, in 1638-9, and it successfully fought off English control.

COOK ISLANDS: former name was *Harvey Islands*. The islands were discovered in 1773 by Captain Cook. They were annexed to *New Zealand* in 1901. In 1962 independence offered by New Zealand was rejected and they achieved internal self-government in September 1965. The group is composed of *Rarotonga*, Mangaia, Aitutaki, Manuae, Takutea, Mitiaro, Atui and Mauke Islands.

COREA: former name of *Korea*.

CORFU (Island): alternative name is *Kerkira*, one of the *Ionian Islands*, part of *Greece*.

CORISCO (Island): in the Bight of Biafra, off the coast of *Rio Muni*, part of *Equatorial Guinea*.

CORNWALLIS (Island): one of the *Parry Islands*, part of *Canada*.

CORSE (Island): alternative name for *Corsica*, Department of *France*.

CORSICA (Island): alternative name for *Corse*, Department of *France*.

COS (Island): alternative name is *Kos*, one of the *Dodecanese Islands*, part of *Greece*.

COSTA RICA: this part of the Caribbean coast was visited by Columbus in 1502, it was conquered by the Spanish in 1563 and given independence in 1821. The area was part of the *Central American Federation* from 1823 to 1838. Full name is *República de Costa Rica*.

COTE D'IVOIRE: alternative name for *Ivory Coast*, in full *République de Côte d'Ivoire*.

COZUMEL (Island): part of *Mexico*.

CRAB (Island): alternative name of *Vieques*, part of *Puerto Rico*.

CRES (Island): former name is *Cherso*, part of *Yugoslavia*.

CRETE (Island): former name is *Candia*, alternative name is *Kriti*, part of *Greece*.

CRIMEA: the region which is now part of the Ukrainian S S R was an independent khanate conquered in the 15th century by the Ottoman

Turks. In 1783 it was annexed by *Russia*. The Crimean War was fought from 1853 to 1856. An independent Crimean Republic was not established until 1917. The republic was dissolved in 1945 after occupation by both the Soviets and Germans and in 1954 it was eventually absorbed into the Ukraine.

CROATIA: one of the six constituent republics of *Yugoslavia* since 1945. There had been an independent Croatia since the 10th century, though the region came under Austro-Hungarian influence from 1878. At Yugoslavia's defeat in 1941, Croatia became a puppet state of the Italians and Germans. The republic includes Slavonia, Dalmatia and most of Istria.

CUBA (Island): full name is *Républica de Cuba*, it was visited by Columbus in 1492. When the Spanish gained a foothold in 1511, it became part of the viceroyalty of *New Spain*. The *USA* occupied the island from 1898 to 1902, and on 20 May 1902 the Republic of Cuba was formed, but many revolutions have occurred since, followed by many constitutions. In 1959 Dr Fidel Castro overthrew the government of General Batista. The Isle of *Youth* is controlled by Cuba.

THE CUMBRAES: two islands in the First of Clyde, within Bute County, part of *Scotland*, part of *UK*.

CURACAO (Island): part of the *Netherlands Antilles*.

CURACAO TERRITORY: former name of *Netherlands Antilles*, prior to 1949.

CURZOLA (Island): former name of *Korcula*, part of *Yugoslavia*, off Dalmatian coast.

CYCLADES ISLANDS: alternative name is *Kikladhes*, part of *Greece*. Composed of *Andros, Naxos, Delos, Syros,* Paros, Tenos, Melos, Kea, Amorgos and Los.

CYPRUS: alternative names are *Kypros* (Greek) and *Kibris* (Turkish). Full names are *Kypriaki Dimokratia* and *Kibris Cumhuriyeti*. The island was a British crown colony from 1925 to 1960, when it became an independent republic (16 August 1960). On 13 February 1975, after an invasion by Turkish troops, the northern part of the island was proclaimed a *Turkish Federated State of Cyprus* within a federal republic of Cyprus.

CYTHERA (Island): former name is *Cerigo*, alternative name is *Kithira*, part of *Greece*.

CZECHOSLOVAKIA: alternative name is Československá S R. This area was once part of the Austro-Hungarian monarchy and declared independence on 28 October 1918. On 11 July 1960 it became the

Czechoslovak Socialist Republic. A federal system of government was set up in October 1968. Czechoslovakia now consists of the Czech Socialist Republic and the Slovak Socialist Republic. Full name is *Československá Socialistická Republika.*

D

DADRA AND NAGAR HAVELI: formerly Portuguese enclaves in *India*, they were integrated as one of the nine union territories of India in 1961.

DAGO (Island): former name of *Khiuma*, part of the *USSR*.

DAHLAK ARCHIPELAGO: composed of Nokra Islands and Dahlak Islands as well as many small uninhabited islands, part of *Ethiopia*.

DAHOMEY: former name of *Benin*. The name changed in 1975.

DAKHIN SHABAZPUR (Island): part of *Bangladesh*.

DANISH WEST INDIES: former name of *Virgin Islands (USA)*. The name changed in 1917 when the islands went to the *USA*.

DANMARK: alternative name for *Denmark*.

DELAWARE: Delaware was the founding state of the *USA*, being the first to ratify the Constitution of the United States in 1787. Originally a territory disputed by the Dutch and English, it became an English colony in 1674 and remained so until the American Revolution of 1775 to 1783.

DELHI: a city and one of the nine union territories of *India*, the Delhi Sultanate dates back to 1192. The city was conquered by Tamerlane in 1398 and enclosed in high stone walls by Shah Jahan in 1638 when he made it the capital of the Mogul Empire. The British took it in 1803. It was a temporary capital of India (1912 to 1931) before New Delhi was given that status.

DELOS (Island): one of the *Cyclades Islands*, part of *Greece*.

DEMOCRATIC KAMPUCHEA: see *Kampuchea*.

DEMOCRATIC REPUBLIC OF AFGHANISTAN: see *Afghanistan*.

DEMOCRATIC REPUBLIC OF THE CONGO: alternative name for *Congo-Kinshasa*, former name of *Zaïre*; name used from 30 June 1960 to 27 October 1971 when it became Zaïre.

DEMOCRATIC REPUBLIC OF MADAGASCAR: see *Madagascar*.

DEMOCRATIC REPUBLIC OF THE SUDAN: see *Sudan*.

DEMOCRATIC REPUBLIC OF VIETNAM: alternative name for *North Vietnam*, former name of northern part of *Vietnam*; the name was used from 1954 to 1976.

DENMARK: full name is *Köngeriget Danmark*. The Danes were involved in Viking raids on Western Europe and England in the 10th century. Thereafter various monarchies have risen to power. Denmark is still a kingdom with various dependencies. Outlying dependencies are: *Bornholm*, *Faroe Islands* and *Greenland*. Local islands are: *Falster*, *Fyn*, *Langeland*, *Lolland*, *Mors*, *Vendsyssel-Thy* and *Zealand*.

D'ENTRECASTEAUX ISLANDS: composed of *Fergusson*, *Goodenough* and *Normanby* islands, part of *Papua New Guinea*.

DEUTSCHE DEMOKRATISCHE REPUBLIK: see *German Democratic Republic*.

DEUTSCHLAND: alternative name for *Germany*.

DEVON (Island): one of the *Parry Islands*, part of *Canada*.

DHODHEKANISOS (Islands): alternative name for *Dodecanese Islands*, part of *Greece*.

DIHEVI RAAJE (Islands): alternative name for the *Maldive Islands*.

DISCO (Island): part of *Greenland*.

DISTRICT OF COLUMBIA: not classified as one of the fifty constituent states of the *USA*, but an independent metropolitan district founded in 1791 which is the seat of the federal capital of Wachington and coextensive with it. In 1871 the city lost its charter and territorial government was transferred to the District of Columbia.

DJAILOLO (Island): former name of *Halmahera*, island in the *Moluccas Group*, part of *Indonesia*.

DJERBA (Island): alternative name is *Jarbah*, part of *Tunisia*.

DJIBOUTI: former names are *French Somaliland* (1881 to 6 July 1967), *Afars and Issas* (6 July 1967 to 27 June 1977). Alternative name is *Jibuti*. The French coast of *Somalia* was occupied in 1881 and the area was renamed the French Territory of the Afars and Issas on 6 July 1967. Independence was gained on 27 June 1977 and the name changed to the *Republic of Djibouti*.

DODECANESE (Islands): alternative name is *Dhodhekanisos*, composed of *Kos*, *Karpathos*, *Rhodes*, and other smaller islands, part of *Greece*, sometimes included in the *Sporadhes* Islands.

DOLAK (Island): alternative name is *Kolepon*, former name is *Frederik Hendrik*. One of the *West Irian Islands*, part of *Indonesia*.

DOMINICA (Island): one of the *Windward Islands* of the *West Indies*. Under British colonial rule from the Napoleonic Wars until 1 March 1967 when it became a member of the *West Indies Associated States* in association with Britain. Independence was achieved on 3 November 1978.

DOMINICAN REPUBLIC: former name is *Santo Domingo*, full name is *República Dominicana*; the Dominican Republic is part of the island of *Hispaniola*. The other part is *Haiti*. Hispaniola was discovered by Columbus in 1492. Spanish rule was established in 1808. The Haitians ruled from 1822 to 1844 and the country was occupied by US marines from 1916 to 1924, although the Dominican Republic was declared independent in 1844. Its present constitution dates from 1966.

DOWLAT AL-KUWAIT: see *Kuwait*.

DRUK-YUL: see *Bhutan*.

DRUMMOND (Island): part of the *USA*.

DUBAI: one of the seven states of the *United Arab Emirates*. A dependency of *Abu Dhabi* until 1833, the skeikdom became a British protectorate and eventually joined the UAE in 1971.

DUCIE (Island): situated between *Pitcairn* and *Easter* Islands. Annexed by United Kingdom in 1902 and now attached to Pitcairn Island.

DUTCH ANTILLES: alternative name for *Netherlands Antilles*.

DUTCH EAST INDIES: former name of *Indonesia*. The name changed when the *Republic of Indonesia* was formed in August 1945.

DUTCH GUIANA: former name of *Surinam*. The name Dutch Guiana was used from 1815 to 25 November 1975.

DUTCH NEW GUINEA: former name of *Irian Jaya* (formerly *West Irian*) part of *Indonesia*.

DUTCH WEST INDIES: alternative name of *Netherlands Antilles*.

E

EAGLE (Island): off the coast of County Mayo, *Irish Republic*.

EAST AFRICA: an unofficial term denoting *Kenya, Uganda, Tanzania, Rwanda* and *Burundi*.

EASTER (Island): alternative (Spanish) name is *Isla de Pascua*, native name is *Rapa Nui*. Situated in the eastern Pacific Ocean between Pitcairn Island and the Chile coast, part of *Chile*.

EASTERN SAMOA (Islands): alternative name for *American Samoa*.

EAST FALKLAND (Island): part of the *Falkland Islands*.

EAST GERMANY: see under full name, *German Democratic Republic*.

EAST INDIES: former name of *Indonesia, Malaysia, Brunei* and the *Philippines*.

EAST PAKISTAN: former name of *Bangladesh*; the name changed on independence on 22 December 1971.

EAST TIMOR: or *Portuguese Timor*, now joined with *West Timor* to become *Timor*. One of the *Lesser Sunda Islands*, part of *Indonesia*.

ECUADOR: known originally by the ancient name of Quito, it was included in the Spanish viceroyalty of *Peru*, then that of *New Granada* in 1717 with modern *Panama, Venezuela* and *Colombia*. Won independence from the Spanish in 1822 when Ecuador joined Colombia to form Greater Colombia. In 1830 Ecuador became an independent republic. Ecuador controls the *Galapagos Islands*. Full name is *República del Ecuador*.

EDGE (Island): part of *Svalbard* island group in Arctic Ocean.

EFATE (Island): alternative name is *Vate*, part of *Vanuatu*, formerly *New Hebrides*.

EGYPT: former name is *United Arab Republic*; this name was used on merging with *Syria* in 1958 until 2 September 1971 (ten years after Syria's secession) when the country resumed the name of Egypt. From 1517 until the 19th century Egypt had been incorporated into the *Ottoman Empire*; On 18 December 1914 the country became a British protectorate until 28 February 1922, when a monarchy was established. In June 1953 the country was declared a republic. The full name is *Arab Republic of Egypt*.

EIMEO (Island): former name of *Moorea*, island in the *Society Islands*, part of *French Polynesia*.

EIRE: alternative name for *Irish Republic*. Also refers to the whole of *Ireland*.

ELBA (Island): part of *Italy*.

EL-DJEMHOURIA EL-DJAZAIRIA: see *Algeria*.

ELEUTHERA (Island): part of the *Bahamas*.

ELLAS: alternative name for *Greece*.

ELLEF RINGNES (Island): part of *Canada*, (Northwest Territory).

ELLESMERE (Island): one of the *Queen Elizabeth Islands*, part of *Canada*.

ELLICE ISLANDS: former name of *Tuvalu*; name changed with independence on 1 October 1978.

ELLINIKI DIMOKRATIA: see *Greece*.

ELOBEY ISLANDS: two islands in Corisco Bay, Gulf of Guinea, part of *Equatorial Guinea*.

EL SALVADOR: full name is *República de El Salvador*. It was a Spanish viceroyalty under *Guatemala* until independence in 1821, then it became part of the *Central American Federation* from 1823 to 1838.

EMPIRE CENTRAFRICAIN: see *Central African Republic*.

ENDERBURY (Island): one of the *Phoenix Islands*, part of *Kiribati*.

ENGLAND: southern part of the Island of Great Britain. In 55 BC Britain was invaded by Julius Caesar and later occupied by the Romans until the 5th century. Angles and Saxons began invasions followed by the Danes in the 9th century. In 1066 the Norman conquest ended the Anglo-Saxon period. Central government was established and the lines of Royal Kings started. Civil wars and conflict with European countries has marked the centuries to modern times. In 1707 England was united with *Scotland* and in 1801 Great Britain and Ireland were united. The *Irish Republic* became independent in 1922 and in 1927 the official name of the united area became the *United Kingdom of Great Britain and Northern Ireland*.

EQUATORIAL GUINEA: full name is *República de Guinea Ecuatorial*, the former name is *Spanish Guinea*. The country is composed of a mainland called *Rio Muni*, sometimes known as Mbini after the former name of the Rio Benito River in the area, and islands called *Bioko* (formerly *Macias Ngumema Biyogo*, and prior to 1973 *Fernando Póo*), *Annobón* (formerly *Pigalu* and before that Annobon), *Corisco*, and *Elobey Islands*. The Spanish province gained self-government in 1963 and independence on 12 October 1968. The name changed from Spanish Guinea to Equatorial Guinea on independence.

ERITREA: federated with and became a province of *Ethiopia* in 1952.

EROMANGA (Island): alternative name is *Erromango*, part of *Vanuatu*, formerly *New Hebrides*.

ERROMANGO (Island): alternative name is *Eromanga*, part of *Vanuatu*, formerly *New Hebrides*.

ESPANA: alternative name for *Spain*.

ESPIRITU SANTO (Island): alternative name is *Santo*, former name is *Marina*; part of *Vanuatu*, formerly *New Hebrides*.

ESTADO ESPANOL: see *Spain*.

ESTADOS UNIDOS MEXICANOS: see *Mexico*.

ESTONIAN SOVIET SOCIALIST REPUBLIC: one of the fifteen constituent republics of the *USSR*. The most northerly of the three independent Baltic Republics of Estonia, *Latvian SSR* and *Lithuanian SSR* between the wars, Estonia was occupied by the Germans in World War II and incorporated into the USSR in 1940.

ETAT COMORIEN: see *Comoro Islands*.

ETHIOPIA: at one time known as Ityopya, former name is *Abyssinia*. Italy was in possession of coastal *Eritrea* from 1882 to 1885. A French Emperor was established in Ethiopia in 1889 who recognized Italian Eritrea. Annexed by Italy in 1935 to form Italian East Africa with Eritrea and *Italian Somaliland*. Ethiopia regained independence in 1941 and Eritrea, as a result of a UN vote in 1950 was joined as a province to Ethiopia in 1952. The *Dahlak* Archipelago is part of Ethiopia.

ETOROFU (Island): former name of *Iturup*, part of the *USSR*.

EUBOEA (Island): alternative name is *Evvoia*, part of *Greece*.

EVVOIA (Island): alternative name for *Euboea*, part of *Greece*.

EZO (Island): or *Yezo*, former name of *Hokkaido*, part of *Japan*.

F

FAEROE ISLANDS: alternative name is *Faroe Islands*.

FAEROERNE: alternative name for *Faroe Islands*.

FADDEI (Island): one of the *New Siberian Islands*, part of the *USSR*.

FAIAL (Island): in the *Azores Islands*, part of *Portugal*.

FAIR ISLE: one of the *Shetland Islands*, in *Scotland*, part of *UK*.

FALKLAND ISLANDS: alternative name is *Islas Malvinas*. The islands were colonized by Britain in 1832. The *Falkland Island Dependencies* used to include *South Georgia, South Sandwich, South Orkney* and *South Shetland*, but in January 1962 the Southern Island groups of South Orkney and South Shetland, were renamed *British Antarctic Territory* along with the British sector of Antarctica and Graham Land. Thus the only remaining Falkland Island Dependencies are now South Georgia and South Sandwich. The Falkland Islands themselves are composed of: *East Falkland, West Falkland* and many smaller islands.

FALKLAND ISLAND DEPENDENCIES: include *South Georgia* and *South Sandwich*, part of *Falkland Islands*.

FALSTER (Island): part of *Denmark*.

FANNING (Island): former name of *Tabuaeran* Island, one of the *Line Islands*, part of *Kiribati*.

FAR EAST: comprises the eastern edge of Asia and adjacent areas, may also include south east Asia, the *Philippines, Indonesia* and Malay Peninsula.

FAROE ISLANDS: alternative names are *Sheep Islands, Faeroe Islands*, or *Faerøerne*. Under Danish rule from 1380. British established protectorate over islands after German occupation (1940). In 1948 home rule was granted. Composed of Stromo and *Ostero* islands plus many smaller ones.

FAYAL (Island): former name of *Faial*, an island in the *Azores Islands*, part of *Portugal*.

FEDERAL AND ISLAMIC REPUBLIC OF THE COMOROS: see *Comoros*.

FEDERAL REPUBLIC OF GERMANY: alternative name is *West Germany*. After the surrender of *Germany* at the end of World War II, the area of pre-war Germany was effectively partitioned into two separate states, although these areas were originally zones of occupation by the Allied Forces. The Federal Republic of Germany came into formal existence on 21 September 1949 and became an independent sovereign state on 5 May 1955. Alternative full name is *Bundesrepublik Deutschland*. *Fehmarn Island* is part of West Germany.

FEDERAL REPUBLIC OF NIGERIA: see *Nigeria*.

FEDERATION OF RHODESIA AND NYASALAND: it was formed in 1953 with *Northern Rhodesia* and *Southern Rhodesia* and *Nyasaland*. Nyasaland and *Northern Rhodesia* withdrew from the Federation in 1963, the former becoming *Malawi*. The self-governing British colony of Southern Rhodesia declared independence in 1965 and became *Zimbabwe* on 17 April 1980.

FEHMARN (Island): part of *Federal Republic of Germany*.

FERGUSSON (Island): one of the *D'Entrecasteaux Islands*, part of *Papua New Guinea*.

FERNANDINA (Island): alternative name is *Narborough*, one of the *Galapagos Islands*, part of *Ecuador*.

FERNANDO PO (Island): former name of *Macias Nguema Biyogo*, present name is *Bioko*, part of *Equatorial Guinea*.

FERRO (Island): alternative name is *Hierro*, island in the *Canary Islands*, part of *Spain*.

FETLAR (Island): one of the *Shetland Islands*, in *Scotland*, part of the *UK*.

FIDJI (Islands): former name of *Fiji*.

FIJI (Islands): former name is *Fidji*. The islands were discovered by Tasman in 1643 and ceded to Britain in 1874. Independence was gained on 10 October 1970. Group composed of *Viti Levu, Vanua Levu*, Taveuni, Kandavu and smaller islands.

FINLAND: alternative name is *Suomi-Finland*. Full names are *Suomen Tasavalta* and *Republiken Finland*. The area was ruled by *Russia* between 1809 and 1917 when a declaration of independence was passed, which was only recognized by Russia in 1920. The *Aland* archipelago is part of Finland.

FLINDERS (Island): one of the *Furneaux Group* of islands northeast of Tasmania, part of *Australia*.

FLORES (Island): one of the *Lesser Sunda Islands*, part of *Indonesia*.

FLORIDA: discovered and colonized by the Spanish, Florida was lost to the British by 1763. It was regained by Spain under the Treaty of Paris in 1783. In 1819 Spain ceded the colony to the *USA* and it was the 17th state to join the Union, in 1845.

FOGO (Island): part of the *Cape Verde Islands*.

FORMENTERA (Island): one of the *Balearic Islands*, part of *Spain*.

FORMOSA (Island): former name of *Taiwan*.

FOX (Islands): composed of *Unimak, Unalaska, Umnak* and *Krenitzen* Islands, in the *Aleutian Islands*, part of the *USA*.

FRANCE: full name is *République Française*. The monarchy of the 18th century was overthrown by the French Revolution and the first empire was founded under Napoleon Bonaparte in 1804. The monarchy was restored in 1815, but not for long. The second republic lasted from 1848 to 1852, and the third was from 1871 to 1940. France was overrun by Germany during the period 1940 to 1944; thus began the fourth republic (1946-1958) after which the fifth republic came into being. Overseas departments of France are the islands of *Corsica, Mayotte, Réunion, Martinique, Guadeloupe, Chesterfield* and *French Guiana*.

FRASER (Island): alternative name for *Great Sandy* Island, part of *Australia*.

FREDERIK HENDRIK (Island): former name of *Dolak*, island in *West Irian*, part of *Indonesia*.

FRENCH CAMEROUN: former name of *Cameroon*.

FRENCH CONGO: see *French Equatorial Africa*.

FRENCH EQUATORIAL AFRICA: an area formed in 1910 with the countries *Gabon, Middle Congo*, and *Ubangi-Shari-Chad*. *Chad* was made a fourth colony apart from Ubangi-Shari in 1920. The countries all gained their independence from France in 1960.

FRENCH ESTABLISHMENTS IN OCEANIA: former name of *French Polynesia*.

FRENCH GUIANA: or *Guiana*, or alternatively *Guyane Française*. The country borders *Brazil*. The French settled in Cayenne in 1643, but in 1676 the area was taken by the Dutch. In 1815 it was retaken by the French. An official penal colony was established from 1854 to 1944. In 1946 the area became a French department. There are a few coastal islands administered by French Guiana, for example *Safety Islands*.

FRENCH GUINEA: former name of *Guinea*. Name changed with independence in 1958.

FRENCH INDOCHINA: former name of *Cambodia, Laos* and *Kampuchea*.

FRENCH MOROCCO: former name of *Morocco*. The name changed in 1956 with independence.

FRENCH OCEANIA: alternatively *French Establishments in Oceania*; both former names of *French Polynesia*.

FRENCH POLYNESIA: includes the *Society Islands, Marquesas Islands, Tubuai Islands*, Gambier Islands, *Tuamotu Islands*. Former names are *French Establishments in Oceania* or *French Oceania*, formed in 1903.

FRENCH SOMALILAND: former name of *Djibouti*. The name French Somaliland was used between 1881 and 1967, then the name *Afars and Issas* was used until 1977 when independence was gained and the name became Djibouti.

FRENCH SOUTHERN AND ANTARCTIC LANDS: part of *Antarctica*. Islands included are *Kerguelen Archipelago* and Crozet.

FRENCH SUDAN: former name of *Mali*. Name changed in 1960 with independence.

FRENCH TERRITORY OF THE AFARS AND ISSAS: former name of *Djibouti*, the name *Afars and Issas* was used between 1967 and 1977.

FRENCH TOGOLAND: former name of *Togo*. Name changed with independence in 1960.

FRENCH WEST AFRICA: federation created 1895 which included *Dahomey* (now *Benin*), *French Guinea* (now *Guinea*), *French Sudan* (now *Mali*), *Ivory Coast, Mauritania, Niger, Senegal* and *Upper Volta* up to their respective independences. Federation dissolved 1959.

FRIENDLY ISLANDS: former name of *Tonga Islands*.

FUERTEVENTURA (Island): one of the *Canary Islands*, part of *Spain*.

FUJAIRAH: one of the seven federated *United Arab Emirates*, it was a British protectorate until it joined the UAE in 1971.

FUNAFUTI (Island): largest island in the *Tuvalu* Group.

FUNEN (Island): former name of *Fyn*, part of *Denmark*.

FURNEAUX GROUP: off the northeast coast of Tasmania. Discovered in 1773 by Captain Furneaux in command of one of Captain Cook's ships. Composed of *Flinders*, Cape Barren, Clarke and many smaller islands, part of *Australia*.

FUTUNA (Islands): part of *Wallis and Futuna Islands*.

FYN (Island): former name is *Funen*, part of *Denmark*.

G

GABON: full name *République Gabonaise*; this area was included in the French Congo in 1886 and became part of *French Equatorial Africa* in 1910. It became the independent Republic of Gabon on 17 August 1960.

GABUN: former name of *Gabon*.

GALAPAGOS ISLANDS: composed of *Fernandina, Isabela, San Salvador, Santa Cruz,* San Cristobal and minor islands, part of *Ecuador*.

GAMBIA: in 1843 The Gambia was declared a British colony. Internal self-government was achieved on 4 October 1963, The Gambia became an independent monarchy on 18 February 1965, and the country became the Republic of Gambia on 24 April 1970.

GARDNER (Island): former name of *Nikumaroro* Island, one of the *Phoenix Islands*, part of *Kiribati*.

GAZA STRIP: between 1917 and 1948 the area was included in the British Mandate of *Palestine*. From 1949 to 1967, apart from November 1956 to March 1957 when under Israeli occupation, the area was administered by *Egypt*. Since 10 June 1967 the area has again been occupied by *Israel*.

GEORGIA: the last of the Thirteen Colonies held by Britain (see *USA*), Georgia was founded in 1733 and became the first Southern State to ratify the Constitution of the United States in 1788. It became the 4th member state of the USA.

GEORGIAN SOVIET SOCIALIST REPUBLIC: one of the fifteen constituent republics of the *USSR*, bordering on the Black Sea. Its ancient names were Colchis (western part) and Iberia. In the 16th century Georgia was divided under Turkish and Persian rule. Between 1801 and 1829 *Russia* acquired all of Georgia and it joined the USSR in 1922 after post-revolutionary independence as part of the Transcaucasian SFSR with *Armenian SSR* and *Azerbaijan SSR*. In 1936 it became a separate republic.

GERMAN DEMOCRATIC REPUBLIC: alternative name is *East Germany*. After the surrender of *Germany* to the Allies in 1945, it was effectively partitioned into two separate states. Former German territories east of the Oder and Neisse rivers including the city of Danzig became part of *Poland*, with the other eastern sections falling under the Russian zone of occupation. Western sections formed the new *Federal Republic of Germany*. East Germany's constitution was enacted in 1949. Its alternative full name is *Deutsche Demokratische Republik*. The GDR owns the islands of *Rugen* and *Usedom*.

GERMAN EAST AFRICA: former name of *Tanzania, Rwanda* and *Burundi.* The area was known as German East Africa during the period 1886 to 1918. After World War I the mandate was given to Britain for *Tanganyika* from 1918 to 1961; subsequently the area became independent and the name changed to Tanzania on unification with *Zanzibar* in 1964. *Belgium* received the mandate of Ruanda-Urundi, and in 1962 each country gained independence and their names changed respectively to *Rwanda* and *Burundi.*

GERMAN KAMERUN: former name of *Cameroon.*

GERMAN SOUTH WEST AFRICA: former name of *Namibia.* German occupation was from 1892 to 1919, after which the mandate was given to *South Africa.* The mandate was terminated by the UN in 1966, and the area was renamed Namibia. South Africa still uses the name *South West Africa.*

GERMANY: after the Franco-Prussian war of 1870-1871 the German Empire was created. After World War I, Germany had to accept the armistice terms of the Versailles Peace Conference and all her colonies were lost. Nazi dictatorship arose in 1933 leading to World War II. After the war territory in the East was lost to *Poland* and the remaining areas were divided into four zones of occupation; American, British, French and Russian. In 1949 the American, British and French zones were reconstituted to form *Federal Republic of Germany* (West Germany) and the Russian zone formed the *German Democratic Republic* (East Germany).

GHANA: former name is *Gold Coast.* In precolonial times the area was composed of the kingdoms of Gonja, Dagomba, Ashanti and Fanti. In 1874 the Ashanti kingdom was defeated by the British and the coastal area colonized as the Gold Coast. In 1901 the northern territories were added to this area under British control. *British Togoland* joined the Gold Coast in 1956 and the whole area became independent *Ghana* on 6 March 1957. It became a republic on 1 July 1960.

GIBRALTAR: the peninsula has been a British crown colony since 1704. *Spain* has claimed the area several times but in 1967 a UN supervised referendum showed that residents reaffirmed their ties with Britain. In April 1980 it was agreed in principle to reopen the frontier by June. This was postponed several times but in December 1982 the new Spanish Government reopened the border to pedestrians.

GILBERT AND ELLICE ISLANDS: former name of *Tuvalu (Ellice Islands)* and *Kiribati (Gilbert Islands).* The British colony of Gilbert and Ellice Islands was formed in 1915 and existed until 1975 when the Ellice Islands withdrew. Tuvalu became independent on 1 October 1978 and Kiribati on 12 July 1979.

GILBERT ISLANDS: former name of the independent republic of *Kiribati*. The islands were split from *Ellice Islands* in 1978. The name change occurred on independence on 12 July 1979.

GOA: formerly a Portuguese enclave in *India*, having been conquered by them in 1510, Goa was integrated into India on 19 December 1961 and with Daman and Diu now comprises one of its nine union territories.

GOKCEADA (Island): former names are *Imbros* or *Imroz*, part of *Turkey*.

GOLD COAST: former name of *Ghana*. The name changed on independence on 6 March 1957.

GOMERA (Island): one of the *Canary Islands*, part of *Spain*.

GONAVE (Island): part of *Haiti*.

GOODENOUGH (Island): former name is *Morata* Island. One of the *D'Entrecasteaux Islands*, part of *Papua New Guinea*.

GOTLAND (Island): part of *Sweden*.

GOZO (Island): part of *Malta*.

GRAHAM (Island): one of the *Queen Charlotte Islands*, part of *Canada*.

GRAND BAHAMA (Island): part of the *Bahamas*.

GRAND CAICOS (Island): alternative name is Middle Caicos, part of the *Turks and Caicos Islands*.

GRAND CANARY (Island): one of the *Canary Islands*, part of *Spain*.

GRAND CAYMAN (Island): part of the *Cayman Islands*.

GRAND-DUCHE DE LUXEMBOURG: see *Luxembourg*.

GRANDE COMORE (Island): part of the *Comoro Islands*.

GRANDE DE GURUPA (Island): alternative name is *Gurupa*, part of *Brazil*.

GRANDE DE TIERRA DEL FUEGO (Island): alternative name for *Tierra del Fuego*, the eastern part belonging to *Argentina* and the western part to *Chile*.

GRANDE-TERRE (Island): part of *Guadeloupe*.

GREAT ABACO (Island): alternative name for *Abaco*, part of the *Bahamas*.

GREAT BRITAIN: see *England*, *Wales*, *Scotland* and *United Kingdom of Great Britain and Northern Ireland*. For Ireland see under *Irish Republic* and *Northern Ireland*.

GREAT INAGUA (Island): alternative name for *Inagua*, part of the *Bahamas*.

GREAT NICOBAR (Island): one of the *Nicobar* Islands in the *Andaman and Nicobar Island* group, part of *India*.

GREAT SANDY (Island): alternative name is *Fraser* Island, off the southeast coast of Queensland, *Australia*, of which it is part.

GREATER ANTILLES (Islands): composed of *Cuba, Jamaica, Hispaniola* and *Puerto Rico*, part of the *West Indies*.

GREATER SUNDA ISLANDS: composed of *Borneo, Sumatra, Java* and *Celebes*; parts of *Indonesia* and *Malaysia*.

GREECE: alternative names are *Ellas* or *Hellas*. Full name is *Elliniki Dimokratia*. Greece has a long and ancient history. Modern Greece became an independent monarchy in 1832. The Bavarian prince who ruled had to abdicate in 1862 and was succeeded by a Danish prince from 1863 to 1913. A republic was established in 1924 but ended with a return to the monarchy in 1935. Italian and German occupation occurred during World War II. The monarchy was abolished in June 1973 when Greece became a presidential republic. Island groups which are part of Greece are the *Ionian Islands, Sporadhes, Dodecanese Islands* and the *Cyclades Islands*. Individual islands administered by Greece are: *Chios, Crete, Cythera,* Euboea, *Lemnos, Lesbos, Samothrace, Thasos Islands.*

GREENLAND (Island): part of the kingdom of *Denmark*; alternative name is *Grønland*. Colonization began in 1721, and Norwegian and Danish trading posts were soon established. In 1951 a Danish-American agreement was signed for the common defence of Greenland. A status of internal autonomy was attained on 1 May 1979. Islands administered by Greenland are *Traill, Disco* and *Milne Land.*

GRENADA (Island): chief of the Grenadine islands in the *Windward Islands*. French settlement began in 1650. The British took over the island in 1783. On 3 March 1967 Grenada became a state in association with Britain. Full independence was achieved on 7 February 1974.

GRONLAND (Island): alternative name of *Greenland*.

GROOTE EYLANDT (Island): part of *Australia*.

GUADALCANAL (Island): part of the *Solomon Islands*.

GUADELOUPE (Island): in 1635 settlement was started by France and it was confirmed as a French possession in 1815. It is now an overseas French department in the *Leeward Islands*. Islands included are the *Marie-Galante*, Les Saintes, *Grande-Terre, Basse-Terre*, Désiderade, St Barthelemy and *St Martin*, of which latter the northern part of the island falls under Guadeloupe administration.

GUAM (Island): it was discovered by Magellan in 1521, belonged to Spain between 1668 and 1898 and taken by the USA in 1898. Some self-government was achieved in 1950 though the island remains an unincorporated territory of the USA. The island is in the *Marianas Island* group.

GUAMBLIN (Island): alternative name is Socorro Island, off the southwest coast of *Chile*, of which it is part.

GUATEMALA: full name is *República de Guatemala*. Central America gained its independence from Spain in 1821 and the *Central American Federation* was formed from 1823 until 1838. Guatemala became a separate nation in 1839 after the collapse of the Central American Federation in 1838. Now known as the Republic of Guatemala, under a constitution adopted in 1965.

GUERNSEY (Island): one of the *Channel Islands*, northwest of Jersey. The dependencies of Guernsey are Alderney, Brechou, *Sark, Herm*, Jethou and Lihou. A *UK* Crown Dependency.

GUIANA : see either *Surinam, Guyana* or *French Guiana*.

GUINEA: former name is *French Guinea*, alternative name is *Guinée*. In 1891 it became a French colony. Independence was gained on 2 October 1958. Full name is République de Guinée.

GUINEA-BISSAU: former name is *Portuguese Guinea*, alternative name is *Guine-Bissau*. First visited by the Portuguese in 1446 but only became an overseas province of Portugal in 1951. After many wars, independence was achieved on 10 September 1974.

GUINEA ECUATORIAL: alternative name is *Equatorial Guinea*.

GUINE-BISSAU: alternative name for *Guinea-Bissau*.

GUINEE: alternative name for *Guinea*.

GUJARAT: one of the twenty-one states of *India*, Gujarat was an independent sultanate from 1401 until its Mogul annexation in 1572. In 1947 it became part of the state of Bombay, and in 1960 a separate state.

GURUPA (Island): alternative name is *Grande de Gurupa*, part of *Brazil*.

GUYANA: former name is *British Guiana*. The settlements of Berbice, Demerara, Essequibo were united as British Guiana in 1831. Self-government was achieved in 1961 and full independence on 26 May 1966 with a name change to Guyana. Republic status was attained in 1970.

GUYANE FRANCAISE: alternative name for *French Guiana*.

H

HADHRAMAUT: or Hadramaut, Hadramawt, former name of area which is now *South Yemen*, in full *People's Democratic Republic of Yemen*.

HAINAN (Island): part of *China*.

HAITI (Island): full name is *République d'Haiti*. Haiti is the western third of the island of *Hispaniola*. *Hayti* is a former name of Hispaniola. Spain ceded Haiti (then called *Saint-Domingue*) to France in 1697, and after many uprisings independence was gained on 1 January 1804, at which stage the name Haiti was used. The US marines occupied the area in 1915 and the US fiscal control only ended on 1 October 1947, although the occupation ended in 1934. *Gonave* and Tortuga Islands are part of Haiti.

HALMAHERA (Island): former name is *Djailolo*, alternative name is *Jailolo*. Island is in the *Moluccas Group*, part of *Indonesia*.

HAN KOOK, see *South Korea*.

HARVEY ISLANDS: former name of *Cook Islands*.

HARYANA: one of the twenty-one states of *India*, created in 1966 out of the Hindi-speaking portion of the *Punjab* state.

HASHEMITE KINGDOM OF THE JORDAN: full name of *Jordan*.

HAUTE-VOLTA: alternative name for *Upper Volta*.

HAWAII (Islands): annexed by the *USA* in 1898, Hawaii was finally admitted to the Union as its 50th state in 1959. The state comprises the eight major islands of Hawaii, *Kauai, Maui, Molokai, Oahu, Lanai, Niihau* and Kahoolawe, as well as other minor islands.

HAYLING (Island): off the southeast coast of Hampshire, *England*. Part of the *UK*.

HAYTI (Island): former name of *Hispaniola*.

HEBRIDES (Islands): alternative name is *Western Islands*, off the coast of *Scotland*, part of *UK*.

HEJAZ: alternative name of *Hijaz*, part of *Saudi Arabia*.

HELLAS: alternative name for *Greece*.

HERM (Island): dependency of *Guernsey* Island, one of the *Channel Islands*, a *UK* Crown dependency.

HERZOGOVINA: alternative spelling for Hercogovina. See *Bosnia and Hercogovina*.

41

HIERRO (Island): alternative name of *Ferro Island*, one of the *Canary Islands*, part of *Spain*.

HIIUMAA (Island): alternative name for *Khiuma*, part of the *USSR*.

HIJAZ: or *Hejaz*. The highland area of *Saudi Arabia* came under Turkish suzerainty in 1517. In 1916 it was proclaimed independent, but it was defeated by the Sultan of *Nejd* who combined the two regions to form the kingdom of Saudi Arabia in 1932.

HIMACHAL PRADESH: one of the twenty-one states of *India*, Himachal Pradesh was made a union territory in 1948 and a state in 1971.

HINN (Island): part of *Norway*.

HISPANIOLA (Island): former name is *Hayti*, now comprises *Haiti* and *Dominican Republic*.

HIVA OA (Island): one of the *Marquesas Islands*, part of *French Polynesia*.

HOKKAIDO (Island): former names are *Ezo, Yezo*, part of *Japan*.

HOLLAND: alternative name for the *Netherlands*.

HOLY (Island): sometimes called Holyhead Island, off the coast of Anglesey County, *Wales* in St George's Channel. Connected to Anglesey Island by a long causeway. Part of the *UK*.

HOLY ISLE: also known as *Lindisfarne*, off the coast of Northumberland, *England*, part of the *UK*.

HOLY SEE: alternative name for *Vatican City*.

HONDO (Island): alternative name for *Honshu*, part of *Japan*.

HONDURAS: independence was gained from Spain in 1821, the area was part of the *Central American Federation* from 1823 to 1838. In full, *República de Honduras*.

HONG KONG: alternative name is *Hsiangchiang*. The area was ceded from *China* to Britain in 1842. In 1898 new territories were leased to Britain for 99 years.

HONSHU (Island): alternative name is *Hondo*, part of *Japan*.

HOORN (Islands): former name of *Futuna* islands, part of *Wallis and Futuna Islands*.

HOSTE (Island): in *Tierra del Fuego* islands, part of *Chile*.

HSIANGCHIANG: alternative name for *Hong Kong*.

HULL (Island): former name of *Orona* Island, one of the *Phoenix Islands*, part of *Kiribati*.

HUNGARY: full name is *Magyar Népköztársaság*. The area was declared an independent republic in April 1849. In 1866 Austria set up an Austro-Hungarian monarchy. After World War I an independent republic was again set up on 17 November 1918. In 1920 however a monarchy was re-established, but in 1941 an alliance was made with Nazi Germany which led to Soviet occupation in 1946. Hungary was proclaimed a people's republic in 1949.

HVAR (Island): former name is *Lesina*, part of *Yugoslavia*.

I

IBIZA (Island): alternative name is *Iviza*. One of the *Balearic Islands*, part of *Spain*.

ICELAND (Island): full name is *Lýdveldid Island*. Under the Danish crown, limited home rule was granted in 1874. In 1918 Iceland became a sovereign state in personal union with *Denmark*. With the German occupation of Denmark in 1940, the UK then the USA sent military forces to protect the island. In 1944 Iceland terminated union with Denmark and was proclaimed an independent republic on 17 June 1944.

IDAHO: admitted as the 43rd state of the *USA* in 1890, it was originally established as a US territory in 1848.

IFNI: former Spanish enclave in *Morocco*. Ifni was ceded by Morocco to *Spain* in 1860, but administration was nominal. Spain returned Ifni to Morocco on 30 June 1969.

ILHA DE COIBA: see *Coiba*.

ILE DE FRANCE: former name of *Mauritius*.

ILES DU SALUT: see *Safety Islands*.

ILLINOIS: the British took possession of the area of Illinois from the indigenous Indians in 1766. It came under North-west Territory from 1787 to 1800, then part of Indiana Territory. It became a separate territory in 1809 and in 1818 the 21st state to join the federal republic of the *USA*.

IMBROS (Island): former name of *Gokceada*, part of *Turkey*.

IMROZ (Island): former name of *Gokceada*, part of *Turkey*.

INAGUA (Island): alternative name is *Great Inagua*, part of the *Bahamas*.

INDEFATIGABLE (Island): alternative name for *Santa Cruz*, one of the *Galapagos Islands*, part of *Ecuador*.

INDIA: alternative name is *Bharat*; full name is *Union of India*. The Portuguese were the first Europeans to land in India in the 15th century, but the British East India Company soon challenged the Portuguese, Dutch and French traders. The British Empire in India began in 1757 and ended with India's independence on 15 August 1947. India became a sovereign republic (though remaining a dominion within the British Commonwealth) when its constitution came into force on 26 January 1950. *Sikkim* and *Kashmir* became Indian protectorates; the former in 1950. In 1974 Sikkim was made an associated state of India. Kashmir is still subject to recurrent hostilities between Indian and Pakistan. India has twenty-one states as follows: *Andhra Pradesh, Assam, Bihar, Gujarat, Haryana, Himachal Pradesh, Jammu and Kashmir,*

Karnataka, Kerala, Madhya Pradesh, Maharashtra, Manipur, Meghalaya, Nagaland, Orissa, Punjab, Rajasthan, Tamil Nadu, Tripura, Uttar Pradesh and West Bengal; and ten union territories: Andaman and Nicobar Islands, Arunachal Pradesh, Chandigarh, Dadra and Nagar Haveli, Delhi, Goa, Laccadive Islands, Mizoram and Pondicherry, and the Island of *Salsette*.

INDIANA: under the Treaty of Paris (1763) the British gained the territory of Indiana from the French. It became part of *Canada* until the end of the American Revolution in 1783. In 1800 Indiana Territory was formed, and it achieved statehood in 1816 as the 19th state to join the confederation of the *USA*.

INDOCHINA: see *French Indochina*.

INDONESIA: in full, *Republic of Indonesia* or *Republik Indonesia*; former names are *Netherlands East Indies* or *Dutch East Indies*. In the 16th century the Portuguese established trading posts in Indonesia. The Dutch came in 1596 and the English in 1600. The Dutch East India Company expanded to control the whole area. The company was liquidated in 1799 and the region became known as the *Netherlands East Indies*. After the Japanese occupation of World War II the area was proclaimed an independent republic in 1949. Indonesia consists of the *Greater Sunda Islands* (the *Kalimantan* area of *Borneo*, *Sumatra*, *Java*, *Celebes*), *Lesser Sunda Islands*, *Moluccas Group*, *Banggai Archipelago*, *West Irian Islands*, plus the isolated islands of *Muna*, *Bangka*, *Billiton*, *Bintan*, *Butung*, *Madura*, *Nias*, *Siberut Simeuleu*, *Talaud*, *Sangi Islands*, *Kawio* and smaller islands.

INNER HEBRIDES (Islands): composed of *Skye*, *Jura*, *Islay*, *Mull* and smaller islands, off the coast of *Scotland*, part of the *UK*.

INNER MONGOLIA: former name of part of *China*.

IONA (Island): one of the *Inner Hebrides*, off the coast of *Scotland*. St Columba landed here from Ireland and it became the centre of early celtic christianity, part of the *UK*.

IONIAN ISLANDS: composed of *Corfu*, *Levkas*, *Cephalonia*, *Zante* and smaller islands, part of *Greece*.

IOWA: originally settled as part of Missouri Territory, Iowa was organized as a separate territory in 1838, becoming in 1846 the 29th member state of the *USA*.

IRAN: former name is *Persia*. Various dynasties over the centuries have ruled Persia, which had been a powerful empire in 500 BC. British and Russian influences in the 19th and 20th centuries caused Persian territory to be lost to neighbouring countries. In 1979 the Shah went into exile and Moslem leaders took control of Iran to convert it to an

Islamic Republic. The Islamic Republic of Iran was proclaimed on 1 April 1979. *Qeshm* Island is administered by Iran.

IRAQ: full name is *Al Jumhouriya al-Iraqia*: the area was known in ancient times as *Mesopotamia*. Iraq was administered by Britain under a League of Nations mandate from 1920 to 1932, although a self-governing kingdom was established in 1921. From 1958 Iraq has been under presidential rule.

IRELAND (Island): consists of the *Irish Republic* and *Northern Ireland*. Alternative name for *Irish Republic*.

IRIAN BARAT (Island): alternative name for *West Irian*, (the western half of *New Guinea*) part of *Indonesia*.

IRIAN JAYA (Island): alternative name for *West Irian*, (the western half of *New Guinea*) part of *Indonesia*.

IRISH REPUBLIC: alternative names are *Eire*, or Republic of Ireland. United with Great Britain in 1801, the Irish Free State was finally established in January 1922 and became the Republic of Ireland on 18 April 1949. Islands included are *Valentia, Aran Islands, Aran, Blasket Islands, Eagle, Achill, Clear Isle*. See also *Northern Ireland*.

ISABELA (Island): alternative name is *Albemarle*, one of the *Galapagos Islands*, part of *Ecuador*.

ISLA DE PASCUA: see *Easter* Island.

ISLAMIC REPUBLIC OF PAKISTAN: see *Pakistan*.

ISLAND (Island): alternative name for *Iceland*.

ISLAS MALVINAS (Islands): alternative name for the *Falkland Islands*.

ISLAY (Island): one of the *Inner Hebrides*, off the coast of *Scotland*, part of the *UK*.

ISRAEL: former name of the area is *Palestine*. After World War I the mandate for Palestine was given to Britain. On 14 May 1948 the *State of Israel* was proclaimed. *Gaza Strip* was included in the British mandate but fell under Egyptian administration for most of 1949 to 1967. The local name for the Gaza Strip is *Qita Ghazzah*. On 5 June 1967 Israel also occupied the *Sinai Peninsula*, the Golan Heights and the *West Bank* of the Jordan. On 25 April 1982 Israel completed its evacuation from Sinai Peninsula and withdrew to the boundary of 1949. Alternative full name is *Medinat Yisrael*.

ITALIA: alternative name for *Italy*.

ITALIAN EAST AFRICA: former name of *Ethiopia*.

ITALIAN SOMALILAND: former name of part of *Somalia*. Italy occupied this area from 1940 to 1941 and 1950 to 1960.

ITALY: alternative name is *Italia*; full name is *Repubblica Italiana*. Unification of the country was achieved between 1848 and 1870 under the monarchy of the House of Savoy. From 1861 to 1922 Italy was governed under a liberal constitution, then replaced by a Fascist dictatorship under Benito Mussolini. In 1946 after World War II the people voted to make the country a republic which came into effect in 1947. In 1929 the *Vatican City* near Rome was proclaimed an independent state with the Pope as absolute ruler. Islands included in Italy are *Elba*, *Sardinia* and *Sicily*.

ITURUP (Island): former name of *Etorufu*. One of the *Kuril Islands*, part of the *USSR*.

ITYOPYA: alternative name for *Ethiopia*.

IVORY COAST: alternative name is *Côte d'Ivoire* or in full, *République de Côte d'Ivoire*. The Portuguese established trading posts in the 16th century and in the later 19th century the French undertook conquests, but did not achieve control until after World War I, when the area became part of *French West Africa*. On 7 August 1960 the area proclaimed independence, having become a republic on 4 December 1958.

IVIZA (Island): alternative name for *Ibiza*, one of the *Balearic Islands*, part of *Spain*.

IWO JIMA (Island): one of the *Volcano Islands*, part of *Japan*.

J

JAILOLO (Island): alternative name for *Halmahera*, island in the *Moluccas Group*, part of *Indonesia*.

JAMAICA (Island): the area was discovered by Columbus in 1494. The British captured the island from the Spanish in 1655. It was formally ceded to England in 1670 and eventually became independent on 6 August 1962.

JAMDENA (Island): former name of *Yamdena*, one of the *Tanimar Islands*, in the *Moluccas Group*, part of *Indonesia*.

JAMES (Island): alternative name for *San Salvador*, one of the *Galapagos Islands*, part of *Ecuador*.

JAMHURIYA KENYA: see *Kenya*.

JAMHUURIYADDA DIMUQRAADIGA SOOMALIA: see *Somalia*.

JAMMU AND KASHMIR: one of the twenty-one states of *India*: Jammu and Kashmir is the greater part of the former Hindu principality of *Kashmir*. The whole of Kashmir came under Indian dominion in 1947 but the area is now in dispute between India and Pakistan.

JAN MAYEN (Island): part of *Norway*.

JAPAN: alternative names are *Nippon* or *Nihon*. The Portuguese first made contact with Japan in 1542. Troubled times continued through various emperors until after World War I when trade and industry expanded. During World War II Japan made a treaty with Russia and occupied many islands and areas in South East Asia, but the Japanese surrendered on 14 August 1945. On 28 April 1952 Japan reassumed full sovereignty. The *Ryukyu Islands* were returned to Japan in 1972, and *Bonin* Islands and *Volcano Islands* in 1968. Japan is composed of *Honshu* (or Mainland), *Kyushu*, *Kokkaido*, *Shikoku* and *Sado*.

JAPEN ISLANDS: in the *West Irian* Islands, part of *Indonesia*.

JARBAH (Island): alternative name for *Djerba*, part of *Tunisia*.

JAVA (Island): alternative name is *Jawa*, one of the *Greater Sunda Islands*, part of *Indonesia*.

JAWA (Island): alternative name for *Java*, one of the *Greater Sunda Islands*, part of *Indonesia*.

JERSEY (Island): island in the *Channel Islands* to the southeast of *Guernsey*, a *UK* Crown dependency.

JESUS (Island): part of *Canada*, (Quebec).

JIBUTI : alternative name for *Djibouti*.

JOHNSTON (Island): discovered by the British in 1807, claimed by the USA in 1858 and became a US naval base in 1941. Part of the *USA*.

JOHORE: one of the eleven federated states of West *Malaysia* on the Malay peninsula, it grew in power with the arrival of Dutch traders in the 17th century. Throughout the 18th century Johore was at war with Bugis usurpers from the *Celebes* and lost its power as a trade centre. Coming under British influence after the creation of the Straits Settlements in 1826, it signed a treaty with Britain in 1885. When the northern states of *Kedah, Kelantan, Perlis* and *Terengganu* were regained by *Siam* from Britain in 1909, Johore joined them to form the Unfederated Malay States, and accepted a British adviser in 1914. After World War II Johore became a member state of the Malayan Union, then of the Federation of *Malaya* in 1948 and the Federation of *Malaysia* in 1963.

JORDAN: former name is *Trans-Jordan*. Alternative names are Urdunn and *Hashemite Kingdom of the Jordan*. The Ottoman Turks gained control of what is now Jordan in 1516 and ruled it until the end of World War I. The area was then mandated to Britain as Trans-Jordan. In 1928 it became a constitutional monarchy and in 1946 it gained its independence. Full name is *Al-Mamlaka al-Urduniya al-Hashemiyah*.

JUAN FERNANDEZ (Islands): group of three islands in the Pacific Ocean. Composed of Más Afuera, Más a tierra (alternatively Robinson Crusoe) and Santa Clara, part of *Chile*.

JUGOSLAVIA: see *Yugoslavia*.

JUMHOURIYA AL-SUDAN AL-DEMOCRATIYA: see *Sudan*.

JUMHOURIYAT AL-YEMEN AL-DIMUQRATIYAH AL-SHA'ABIAH: see *Yemen*.

JURA (Island): one of the *Inner Hebrides*, off the coast of *Scotland*, part of *UK*.

K

KABINDA: see *Cabinda*.

KAI ISLANDS: also known as the Kei Islands, a group in the *Moluccas Group*, comprises the Great Kai, Little Kai and many smaller islands, part of *Indonesia*.

KAISER-WILHELMSLAND: German name for northern section of *New Guinea* colonized by Germans from 1884 to 1914.

KALIMANTAN (Island): part of *Borneo* one of the *Greater Sunda Islands*. Kalimantan is under the government of *Indonesia*.

KAMARAN (Island): part of *South Yemen* since 1967.

KAMERUN: former name of *Cameroon*, when a German colony.

KAMPUCHEA: full name is *Democratic Kampuchea*, alternative name *Cambodia*. Formerly known as part of *French Indochina*, the area was a French protectorate from 1863 to 1867, when it was reorganized by *Siam* under French control. Cambodia became a constitutional monarchy in 1947 and an Associate State of the French Union in 1949. It gained independence in 1953 and severed all remaining links with France, *Vietnam* and *Laos* in 1955. On 9 October 1970 the kingdom of Cambodia was renamed the *Khmer Republic*. The Khmer Rouge took power in 1975 and the country became known as Kampuchea on 21 March 1977.

KANGAROO (Island): part of *Australia*, (South Australia).

KANSAS: designated Indian territory in the early 19th century, Kansas became a territory of the *USA* in 1854 and became its 34th member state in 1861.

KARAFUTO (Island): former name of *Sakhalin*, part of *USSR*.

KARAGIN (Island): part of the *USSR*.

KARNATAKA: one of the twenty-one states of *India*, it was conquered by the Delhi Sultanate in 1313 and transferred from Hindu to Moslem hands in the late 18th century. The British took Karnataka in 1799 and it joined the Union of India in 1947 as part of Hyderabad state. It became a separate state in 1956.

KARPATHOS (Island): former name is *Scarpanto*, one of the *Dodecanese Islands*, part of *Greece*.

KASHMIR: a former Hindu principality now divided between *India* and *Pakistan*. The larger part is known as *Jammu and Kashmir*; the area known as Azad Kashmir is controlled by Pakistan.

KATANGA: in July 1960 after the *Democratic Republic of the Congo* became independent the area of Katanga proclaimed its independence. Two and a half years later by 14 January 1963 the UN ended the Katanga secession, at a later stage the area became the Shaba Province of *Zaïre*.

KATAR: alternative name of *Qatar*.

KAUAI (Island): one of the *Hawaii Islands*, part of the *USA*.

KAWIO (Islands): northeast of the Celebes, composed of many small islands, part of *Indonesia*.

KAZAKH SOVIET SOCIALIST REPUBLIC: or Kazakhstan. One of the fifteen constituent republics of the *USSR*. Although rebelling against Russian domination in 1916, the Kazakhs were grouped as the Kazakh Autonomous SSR in 1925 and joined the USSR in 1936.

KEDAH: one of the eleven federated states of *West Malaysia* on the Malay peninsula, it was under nominal control by the Siamese from the 16th century and was formally ceded to *Siam* by the British in 1826. In 1909 the four northern states of Kedah, *Kelantan, Perlis* and *Terengganu* were regained by Britain and, with *Johore*, became the Unfederated Malay States. After World War II Kedah became a member state of the Malayan Union, then the Federation of *Malaya* in 1948 and the Federation of Malaysia in 1963.

KEELING ISLANDS: alternative name of *Cocos Islands*.

KEFALLINIA (Island): alternative name for *Cephalonia*, one of the *Ionian Islands*, part of *Greece*.

KELANTAN: one of the eleven federated states of West *Malaysia* on the Malay peninsula, it was one of the four most northerly kingdoms which fell under Siamese influence from the 16th century. Under the Anglo-Siamese Treaty of 1826 it remained under Siamese control but was regained by Britain in 1909. With the other northern states of *Kedah, Perlis* and *Terengganu* (and *Johore*), it became one of the Unfederated Malay States. After World War II Kelantan joined the Malayan Union, then the Federation of *Malaya* in 1948 and the Federation of Malaysia in 1963.

KENTUCKY: settled in the mid-18th century, Kentucky became a county of *Virginia* in 1776 and a separate state in 1792, the 15th to join the Union of the *USA*.

KENYA: formerly part of *British East Africa*. Agreement between Britain and Germany in 1886 led to Britain controlling Kenya. The Mau-Mau uprising between 1952 and 1956 against British rule led to greater home rule and independence on 12 December 1963. In 1964 it became an independent republic. Full name is *Jamhuriya Kenya*.

KERALA: one of the twenty-one states of *India*, Kerala was created in 1956 from the princely states of Cochin and Travancore and areas formerly in the presidency of Madras.

KERGUELEN ARCHIPELAGO: part of *Antarctica*.

KERKIRA (Island): alternative name for *Corfu*, one of the *Ionian Islands*, part of *Greece*.

KERMADEC ISLANDS: islands in the southwest Pacific Ocean, north of New Zealand. Largest island is Sunday Island or Raoul Island. Annexed to *New Zealand* in 1887.

KHIOS (Island): alternative name of *Chios*, part of *Greece*.

KHIUMA (Island): alternative name is *Hiiumaa*, former name is *Dago*, part of the *USSR*.

KHMER REPUBLIC: name used for what is now *Kampuchea* between 1970 and 1977. Before 1970 the country was known as *Cambodia*, formerly part of *French Indochina*.

KIBRIS (Island): alternative (Turkish) name for *Cyprus*.

KIBRIS CUMHURIYETI: see *Cyprus*.

KIKLADHES (Islands): alternative name is *Cyclades Islands*, part of *Greece*. Composed of *Andros, Naxos, Delos, Syros*, Paros, Tenos, Melos, Kea, Amorgos, Los and other small islands.

KING (Island): part of *Australia*, (Tasmania).

KING (Island): part of *Canada*, (British Columbia).

KING WILLIAM (Island): part of *Canada*, (Northwest Territory).

KIRGHIZ SOVIET SOCIALIST REPUBLIC: or Kirghizia. In 1924 a Kara-Kirghiz autonomous province was formed within the Russian Soviet Federated Socialist Republic. In 1926 it became an autonomous republic and in 1936 one of the constituent republics of the *USSR*.

KIRIBATI (Islands): former name is *Gilbert Islands*, name changed with independence on 12 July 1979. The islands were made a British protectorate in 1892 and a colony with the Ellice Islands in 1915. Independence was attained in July 1979. The group is composed of the *Line Islands*, the *Phoenix Islands, Tarawa, Banaba, Butaritari*, and smaller islands.

KIRIMATI (Island): former name is *Chistmas* Island, one of the Line Islands, part of *Kiribati*.

KISHM (Island): former name of *Qeshm*, part of *Iran*.

KITHIRA (Island): alternative name for *Cythera*, part of *Greece*.

KIUSHU (Island): alternative name for *Kyushu*, part of *Japan*.

KODIAK (Island): part of the *USA*, (Alaska).

KOLEPON (Island): alternative name for *Dolak*, one of the *West Irian* Islands, *part of Indonesia*.

KOLGUYEV (Island): part of the *USSR*, (southwest of Novaya Zemlya).

KOMSOMOLETS (Island): one of the *Severnaya Zemlya Islands*, part of the *USSR*.

KONGERIGET DANMARK: see *Denmark*.

KONGERIKET NORGE: see *Norway*.

KONGO: former name of *Zaïre*, europeanaized to *Congo*.

KONINKRIJK BELGIE: see *Belgium*.

KONINKRIJK DER NEDERLANDEN: see *Netherlands*.

KONUNGARIKET SVERIGE: see *Sweden*.

KORCULA (Island): former name is *Curzola*, part of *Yugoslavia*.

KOREA: former names are *Chosen* and *Corea*. In 1910 Japan formally annexed the country and held it until 1945. At the end of World War II Korea was divided into two zones with Soviet troops in the north and American troops to the south of the latitude $38°N$. In 1948 two separate regimes were formally established, the *Republic of Korea* in the south and the *People's Democratic Republic of Korea* in the north.

KOS (Island): alternative name is *Cos*. One of the *Dodecanes Islands*, part of *Greece*.

KOTELNYY (Island): one of the *New Siberian Islands*, part of the *USSR*.

KRENITZEN (Islands): a group in the *Fox* Islands, part of the *USA*. Composed of Akutan and Akun plus three smaller islands.

KRITI (Island): alternative name for Crete, part of *Greece*.

KRK (Island): former name is *Veglia* Island, part of *Yugoslavia*.

KUIU (Island): in the *Alexander Archipelago*, part of the *USA*.

KUNASHIR (Island): one of the *Kuril Islands*, part of the *USSR*.

KUNGHIT (Island): one of the *Queen Charlotte Islands*, part of *Canada*.

KUPREANOF (Island): in the *Alexander Archipelago*, part of the *USA*.

KURIA MURIA (Islands): part of *Oman* since 1967. Before 1967 it was part of *Aden*. Composed of Hasikiya, Suda, Hallaniya, Qibliya, Gharzaut.

KURIL ISLANDS: composed of *Paramushir, Iturup, Kunashir* and Urup Island. Part of the *USSR*.

KUSAIE (Island): one of the *Caroline Islands*, part of the *Pacific Islands (USA)*.

KUWAIT: full name is *Dowlat al-Kuwait*. The area was settled by the Arabs in the 18th century. In 1899 due to fear of Turkish rule, the ruling Sheikh made Kuwait a British protectorate. In June 1961 the protectorate was ended but British troops were provided when *Iraq* claimed sovereignty over Kuwait. *Bubiyan* island is part of Kuwait.

KUWAYT: alternative name for *Kuwait*.

KWAJALEIN (Island): part of the *Ralik Chain* in the *Marshall Islands*, part of the *Pacific Islands (USA)*.

KYPRIAKI DIMOKRATIA: see *Cyprus*.

KYPROS (Island): alternative (Greek) name for *Cyprus*.

KYUSHU (Island): alternative name is *Kiushu*, part of *Japan*.

L

LAALAND (Island): former name of Lolland, part of *Denmark*.

LACCADIVE ISLANDS: one of the nine union territories of *India*. Composed of Androth, Kavaratti, Minicoy, Amindivi and smaller islands.

LAKSHADWEEP: Union Territory of the islands groups of *Laccadive*, Minicoy, and Amindivi.

LA MADDALENA (Island): one of the islands off the coast of *Sardinia*, part of *Italy*. *Caprera* Island is connected by a causeway.

LANAI (Island): one of the *Hawaii Islands*, part of *USA*.

LANGELAND (Island): part of *Denmark*.

LANZAROTE (Island): one of the *Canary Islands*, part of *Spain*.

LAO PEOPLE'S DEMOCRATIC REPUBLIC: see *Laos*.

LAOS: full name is *Lao People's Democratic Republic*. In 1707 internal strife brought about a split into northern and southern Laos. After French explorations in the 19th century, Laos came under French protection as part of *French Indochina*. The area was reunited into a monarchy in 1947 and in 1949 Laos became semi-autonomous within the French Union, to gain full sovereignty by 1953. A ceasefire from the Vietnam War was declared in 1973 and a coalition government was inaugurated in 1974. Influence from Cambodia and Vietnam led to the fall of the monarchy on 3 December 1975 and the pro-Western populace fled to *Thailand*. It was declared a republic in December 1975.

LA PALMA (Island): one of the *Canary Islands*, part of *Spain*.

LATVIAN SOVIET SOCIALIST REPUBLIC: one of the fifteen constituent republics of the *USSR*. From 1921 to 1940 it was one of the three independent Baltic Republics of *Estonian SSR*, Latvia and *Lithuanian SSR*, having gained independence in 1921. The republic was occupied by Russia in 1940.

LAVONGAI (Island): alternative name for *New Hanover*; an island in the *Bismarck Archipelago*, part of *Papua New Guinea*.

LEBANON: full name is *Al-Joumhouriyat al-Loubnaniat*, alternative name is *Lubnan*. Conflict between religious communities led to the intervention of the French in 1861, and the Ottoman sultan was forced to appoint a Christian governor. After World War I the area fell under a French mandate. The country was proclaimed an independent republic on 1 January 1944.

LEEWARD ISLANDS: the Leeward Island colony defederated in 1956. The group is composed of *Virgin Islands, Guadeloupe, St Eustatius, Saba, St Martin, Antigua and Barbuda, St Kitts-Nevis, Anguilla* and *Montserrat*.

LEMNOS (Island): alternative name is *Limnos*, part of *Greece*.

LESBOS (Island): alternative names are *Mytilene*, or *Lesvos*, sometimes included in the *Sporadhes* Islands, part of *Greece*.

LESINA (Island): former name of *Hvar*, part of *Yugoslavia*.

LESOTHO: former name is *Basutoland*, after wars with Zulu and Boers, Moshesh put his country under the protection of the British as a crown colony in 1868. In 1871 it was annexed by the *Cape of Good Hope* colony but in 1884 it fell directly under Britain. After the formation of the *Union of South Africa* in 1910, Basutoland became a High Commission territory. On 4 October 1966 it gained independence and changed its name to Lesotho.

LESSER ANTILLES: composed of *Leeward Islands, Windward Islands, Trinidad and Tobago* and *Barbados*.

LESSER SUNDA ISLANDS: composed of *Bali, Lombok, Sumbawa, Sumba, Flores,* Solar islands, *Alor* and *Timor*, part of *Indonesia*.

LES VALLEES D'ANDORRE: see *Andorra*.

LESVOS (Island): alternative name for *Lesbos*, part of *Greece*.

LEUCAS (Island): former name is *Santa Maura*, alternative name is *Levkas*, one of the *Ionian Islands*, part of *Greece*.

LEVANT: former name of part of the *Near East*, now the *Middle East*.

LEVKAS (Island): alternative name for *Leucas*, one of the *Ionian Islands*, part of *Greece*.

LEWIS WITH HARRIS: one of the *Outer Hebrides*, off the coast of *Scotland*, part of the *UK*.

LEYTE (Island): one of the *Visayan Islands*, part of the *Philippines*.

LIBERIA: the area was founded in 1821 when Americans were granted possession of Cape Mesurado. On 26 July 1847 the area was declared independent.

LIBYA: full names are *Socialist People's Libyan Arab Republic* and *Al-Jamahiriyah al-Arabia al-Libya al-Shabiya al-Ishtirakiya*. Ottoman rule controlled much of the area, as did the soldiers of slave origins. The Turko-Italian war of 1911-1912 left the country with little development. In 1934 Italy adopted the name Libya for the colony and in

1949 the UN had jurisdiction. On 24 December 1951 the country became independent as the United Kingdom of Libya. Revolution established the Libyan Arab Republic on 1 September 1969. It became the Socialist People's Libyan Arab Republic in 1977.

LIECHTENSTEIN: the principality was created in 1719. Liechtenstein became independent in 1866 after having been a member of the German Confederation from 1815 to 1866. Since 1919 Liechtenstein has been represented abroad through *Switzerland*.

LIFOU (Island): alternative name is *Lifu*, one of the *Loyalty Islands*, part of *New Caledonia*.

LIFU (Island): alternative name for *Lifou*, one of the *Loyalty Islands*, part of *New Caledonia*.

LIMNOS (Island): alternative name for *Lemnos*, part of *Greece*.

LINDISFARNE (Island): also known as *Holy Isle*, off the coast of Northumberland, part of the *UK*.

LINE ISLANDS: composed of Flint, Vostok, Caroline, Starbuck, Malden, Jarvis, Palmyra, *Kirimati, Fabuaeran, Teraina*, part of *Kiribati*.

LITHUANIAN SOVIET SOCIALIST REPUBLIC: one of the fifteen constituent republics of the *USSR*. A large state which in 1569 was united with *Poland* until the Lithuanian Kingdom was recognized by the Germans in 1918, but as one of the three independent Baltic Republics remained at war with Russia until 1920. After a mutual assistance pact with the USSR in 1939, Lithuania became incorporated as a Soviet Socialist Republic in 1940.

LOFOTEN ISLANDS: group in the Norwegian Sea off the coast of Nordland County. Main Islands are Austvågøy, Vestvågøy and Moskenes, part of *Norway*.

LOLLAND (Island): former name is *Laaland*, part of *Denmark*.

LOMBOK (Island): one of the *Lesser Sunda Islands*, part of *Indonesia*.

LONG (Island): part of the *USA*, (Massachusetts).

LONG (Island): part of the *Bahamas*.

LORD HOWE (Islands): former name for *Ontong Java Islands*, part of *Solomon Islands*.

LOUISIADE ARCHIPELAGO: composed of *Tagula*, Rossel, Misima, Deboyne, part of *Papua New Guinea*.

LOUISIANA: settled by the Creoles, the Spanish and French, Louisiana in the 17th century occupied a much greater area than at present. During the 18th century it came under successive British and Spanish influences until it was claimed by Napoleon in 1802. Napoleon sold Louisiana to the *USA* in 1803 and in 1804 it was divided into two areas. The southern half was admitted to the Union as its 18th member state in 1812.

LOYALTY ISLANDS: composed of *Lifou, Mare* and Uvea, part of *New Caledonia*.

LUBNAN: alternative name for *Lebanon*.

LUING (Island): one of the *Inner Hebrides*, off the coast of *Scotland*, part of the *UK*.

LUNDY (Island): island in the Bristol Channel, off the coast of Devonshire, part of the *UK*.

LUTZELBURG: alternative name for *Luxembourg*.

LUXEMBOURG: or *Luxemburg*; alternative name is *Lutzelburg*. Full name is *Grande-Duché de Luxembourg*. The area passed from Spanish to Austrian rule in 1714 and was ceded to *France* in 1797. It was made a grand duchy in union with the *Netherlands* in 1815. The main part of this duchy was obtained by *Belgium* in 1839, and the remaining part became a possession of the Dutch royal family. In 1867 Luxembourg was declared a neutral territory and Prussian forces withdrew. Germany occupied the area in both world wars. In 1922 the grand duchy formed a customs union with *Belgium*.

LUZON (Island): part of the *Philippines*.

LYAKHOVSKIY (Island): one of the *New Siberian Islands*, part of the *USSR*.

LYDVELDID ISLAND: see *Iceland*.

M

MACAO: former name is *Aomen*; alternative name is *Macau*. It was first visited by Vasco da Gama in 1497 and a trading post was established in 1557. In 1849 Portugal proclaimed the area as a free port. It remains a Portuguese overseas territory.

MACAU: alternative name of *Macao*.

MACEDONIA: one of the six constituent republics of *Yugoslavia* since 1945. Not to be confused with the name Macedonia as applied to the whole region of ancient Macedon, covering a crescent shape across *Greece*, Yugoslavia and *Bulgaria*.

MACIAS NGUEMA BIYOGO (Island): former name is *Fernando Po*, and the present name is *Bioko*, part of *Equatorial Guinea*.

MACKENZIE KING (Island): part of *Canada*, (Northwest Territory).

MACQUARIE (Island): in the Pacific Ocean off the southeast coast of *Tasmania*, of which it is part.

MADAGASCAR: former name is *Malagasy Republic*. In the 1800s the French occupied Madagascar and established a protectorate over the area in 1885. On 14 October 1958 the country became autonomous within the French community and was renamed the Malagasy Republic. Full independence was achieved 26 June 1960. In December 1975 the country accepted a new constitution and with that became known as the *Democratic Republic of Madagascar*.

MADEIRA ISLANDS: composed of Madeira, Porto Santo and smaller islands, part of *Portugal*.

MADHYA PRADESH: one of the twenty-one states of *India*, Madhya Pradesh was occupied by the British in 1820. From 1903 to 1950 the state was known as Central Provinces and Berar.

MADOERA (Island): former name of *Madura*, part of *Indonesia*.

MADRE DE DIOS ARCHIPELAGO: group of islands off the southwest coast of *Chile*, of which they are part.

MADURA (Island): former name is *Madoera*, part of *Indonesia*.

MAGDALEN ISLANDS: group of islands in the Gulf of St Lawrence, part of Quebec, *Canada*.

MAGDALENA (Island): in the south between the Chonos Archipelago and the Chile coast, part of *Chile*.

MAGHRIB: alternative name for *Morocco*.

MAGYAR NEPKOZTARSASAG: see *Hungary*.

MAHARASHTRA: one of the twenty-one states of *India*, Maharashtra was incorporated by the British into the Bombay presidency in the early 19th century. In 1960 Bombay was split into the two states of Maharashtra and *Gujarat*.

MAHE (Island): part of *Seychelles*.

MAINE: contested by the French and British during the 17th and 18th centuries, Maine won independence in the American Revolution and it was admitted to the *USA* as a state in 1820.

MAINLAND (Island): alternative name for *Pomona*, one of the *Orkney Islands* in *Scotland*, part of *UK*.

MAINLAND (Island): one of the *Shetland Islands* in *Scotland*, part of *UK*.

MAINLAND CHINA: alternative name for *China*.

MAIO (Island): former name is *Mayo*, part of the *Cape Verde Islands*.

MAJORCA (Island): alternative name is *Mallorca*, one of the *Balearic Islands*, part of *Spain*.

MAKIN (Island): former name of *Butaritari* Island, part of *Kiribati*.

MAKIRA (Island): alternative name for *San Cristobal*, part of the *Solomon Islands*.

MALACCA: alternative name is *Melaka*; one of the eleven federated states of West *Malaysia* on the Malay peninsula. The Malacca Sultanate of the 15th century was the first of the powerful Malay Kingdoms. It fell first to the Portuguese (1511) then to the Dutch (1641) and was occupied by the British in 1795. From 1818 to 1824 it temporarily reverted to the Dutch. In 1826 Malacca was joined with *Pinang* and *Singapore* to form the British colony of the Straits Settlements. After World War II the Straits Settlements merged with the Malayan Union and Malacca subsequently became a member state of the Federation of *Malaya* in 1948 and the Federation of Malaysia in 1963.

MALAGASY REPUBLIC: former name of *Madagascar*.

MALAITA (Island): part of the *Solomon Islands*.

MALAWI: formerly the *Nyasaland* protectorate. Britain proclaimed the Shire Highlands as a protectorate in 1889. In 1891 the present day Malawi was called British Central African Protectorate. In 1907 this was changed to Nyasaland until 1964. In 1953 Nyasaland joined the *Federation of Rhodesia and Nyasaland* but withdrew in 1959. On 6 July 1966 Malawi became an independent republic.

MALAYA: the area of southern Asia which includes southern *Thailand* and *Peninsular Malaysia*, part of *Malaysia*. Now *West Malaysia*.

MALAY ARCHIPELAGO: includes *Indonesia, Malaysia, Brunei, Philippines.*

MALAYSIA: composed of *Malaya,* (excluding *Singapore*), *Sarawak* and *Sabah.* Malaya's former names are *British Malaya, West Malaysia* and *Peninsular Malaysia,* and the alternative name is Semenanjung Malaysia. The former name of Sabah is *British North Borneo* or *North Borneo.* In 1786 British trade began in the area and Singapore was founded in 1819. Malacca was acquired from the Dutch in 1824, and the Malay peninsula came under British influence. A joint administration was formed in 1826 for Pinang, Malacca and Singapore, known as the Straits Settlements. During World War II the area was occupied by the Japanese and in 1946 when the British returned a Malayan Union was formed of all the Peninsular possessions. After much opposition the Federation of Malaya was formed in 1948. It now comprises eleven Malay States and the Federal Territory of Kuala Lumpur. The states are *Johore, Kedah, Kelantan, Malacca, Negri Sembilan, Pahang, Perak, Perlis, Pinang, Selangor* and *Terengganu.* In 1957 the Federation became independent within the Commonwealth and on 16 September 1963 Singapore, Sabah and Sarawak were added to the Federation, thus creating the Federation of Malaysia. Singapore seceded from Malaysia on 9 August 1965.

MALDIVE ISLANDS: alternative name is *Dihevi Raaje,* full name is *Republic of the Maldives.* In 1887 these islands became a protected state of Britain, with a ruling Sultan. They obtained independence as a sultanate on 26 July 1965 and in 1968 this dynasty was ended and a republic declared.

MALEKULA (Island): alternative name is *Mallicolo,* part of *Vanuatu,* formerly *New Hebrides.*

MALI: full name is *République du Mali;* former name is *French Sudan* or *Soudan.* In the 19th century Moslems opposed a French invasion, but were finally conquered in 1898. The area became known as French Sudan, and part of *French West Africa.* On 24 November 1958 the area voted to join the French Community as the autonomous Sudanese Republic. On 4 April 1960 the area joined the Mali Federation with the Republic of Senegal and was granted independence, but the Federation was dissolved in August 1960. Mali was proclaimed a fully independent republic on 22 September 1960.

MALLICOLO (Island): alternative name for *Malekula,* part of *Vanuatu.*

MALLORCA (Island): alternative name for *Majorca,* one of the *Balearic Islands,* part of *Spain.*

MALPELO (Island): in the eastern Pacific Ocean off the coast of *Colombia* of which it is part.

MALTA: full name is *Republikka Ta Malta*; the islands were under Napoleonic rule until the British ousted the French in 1800. Independence was achieved on 21 September 1964 and Malta became a republic on 13 December 1974. Islands included in the state are Malta, *Gozo* and Comino.

MALUKU (Islands): alternative name for *Moluccas Group*, part of *Indonesia*.

MALVINA DEL ESTE (Islands): alternative name for *West Falkland Islands*.

MAN (Isle of): lies in the Irish sea off the coast of Cumbria, England. It is a dependency of the Crown with considerable self government. The *United Kingdom* is responsible for defence and international relations.

MANCHUKUO: the Japanese invaded Manchuria in 1931 and founded Manchukuo in 1932. It remained an independent state under Japanese military control until 1949 when Chinese sovereignty was reasserted. It is now a section of *Manchuria*, part of *China*.

MANCHURIA: the area known by this name is smaller than it was in the 19th century. In 1860 territory was lost to Siberia and in 1955 areas were taken over by *Mongolia*. Japan and Russia have fought over the region. Russia was dominant from 1898 to 1904, Japan took control of the southern half from 1905 to 1931, and occupied the whole area against Chinese military resistance from 1931 to 1949 with certain areas independent, such as the *Manchukuo* state. From 1949 to 1954 Manchuria was ruled by *China* under a communist regime. The area continues to be ruled by China.

MANHATTAN (Island): part of New York, *USA*.

MANIPUR: one of the twenty-one states of *India*, Manipur was part of *Assam* until it became a union territory in 1947. It achieved statehood in 1972.

MANITOBA: one of the twelve constituent provinces of *Canada*, it was sold by the Hudson's Bay Company to the confederation of Canada in 1870. Its area was enlarged in 1881 and in 1912 it was extended to Hudson Bay.

MANITOULIN (Island): in the northern part of Lake Huron, part of Ontario, *Canada*.

MANRA (Island): former name is *Sydney* Island, one of the *Phoenix Islands*, part of *Kiribati*.

MANSEL (Island): part of *Canada*, (Northwest Territory).

MANUS (Islands): alternative name is *Admiralty* Islands, part of *Papua New Guinea*.

MAPIA ISLANDS: alternative name is Saint David Islands, in the western Pacific Ocean north of Irian Barat. Occupied by US forces 15 November 1944.

MARAJO (Island): part of *Brazil*.

MARE (Island): one of the *Loyalty Islands*, part of *New Caledonia*.

MARGARITA (Island): part of *Venezuela*.

MARIANAS ISLANDS: these islands were nominally Spanish until 1898 when they were sold to Germany, with the exception of *Guam* which was ceded to the USA. In 1914 Japan seized the islands from Germany and they were mandated to Japan in 1920. US forces occupied the Marianas in World War II and the group became part of the *Pacific Islands (USA)*. Guam island is independent. Other large islands in the group are *Tinian* and *Saipan*. The Northern Marianas Islands fall under a covenant made on 24 March 1976 to establish a Commonwealth of the Northern Marianas Islands which will become fully effective on termination of the US trusteeship.

MARIE-GALANTE (Island): part of *Guadeloupe*.

MARINA (Island): former name of *Espiritu Santo*, part of *Vanuatu*.

MARQUESAS ISLANDS: composed of *Hiva Oa*, Fatu Huku, Tehvata, Motane, Fatu Hiva, *Nuku Hiva*, Hatutu, Eiao, Motu Iti, Va Huka, Va Pou, part of *French Polynesia*.

MARROCCO: former name of *Morocco*.

MARCH (Island): part of *USA*, (Louisiana).

MARSHALL ISLANDS: composed of the *Ratak* and *Ralik Chains*. Explored by British navigators Gilbert and Marshall in 1788. Claimed by Germany in 1885, invaded and seized by Japan in 1914 with a mandate granted in 1920. Invaded in 1944 by the USA and became part of the US Trust territory in 1947.

MARTHA'S VINEYARD (Island): part of *USA*, (Massachusetts).

MARTINIQUE (Island): one of the *Windward Islands* in the *West Indies*. French colonization began in 1653 and it became a department of France in 1946.

MARYLAND: one of the original Thirteen Colonies (see *USA*), it was settled by English Puritans in the 17th century and became a crown colony in 1688. In 1783 it gained independence and five years later became the 7th state to join the Union.

MASBATE (Island): one of the *Visayan Islands*, part of the *Philippines*.

MASCARENE ISLANDS: composed of *Réunion, Mauritius,* and *Rodrigues.*

MASSACHUSETTS: settlement of this historic state of the *USA* began when the Pilgrims arrived in the Mayflower in 1620. In 1629 the Massachusetts Bay Colony was established. Under English Puritan influence for over a century, Massachusetts was at the crux of the American Revolution after the Boston Tea Party rebellion of 1773. After gaining independence it became the 6th member state of the Union in 1788.

MAUI (Island): one of the *Hawaiian Islands*, part of *USA.*

MAURITANIA: full name is *République Islamique de Mauritanie.* From the 17th century Dutch, British and French traders were active along the southern Mauritanian coast. France gained control of the area in the late 19th century and declared the region a protectorate in 1903. In 1920 it became separated from *Senegal* as a colony in *French West Africa.* The Republic of Mauritania elected on 28 November 1958 to remain within the French Community as an autonomous republic. It became fully independent on 28 November 1960.

MAURITIUS: former name is *Île de France.* The area was occupied by the Dutch from 1598 to 1710 and named after Prince Maurice of Nassau. The French settled on the island in 1722 and renamed it Île de France. During the Napoleonic Wars Britain captured the island and restored the Dutch name Mauritius. The island was a crown colony from 1810 to 12 March 1968 when it gained independence. *Rodrigues, Agalega* and St Brandon islands are part of Mauritius, in the *Mascarene Islands.*

MAYO (Island): former name of *Maio*, part of *Cape Verde Islands.*

MAYOTTE (Island): one of the *Comoro Islands.* Mayotte remained under French jurisdiction after the Comoro Islands declared independence.

MEDINAT YISRAEL: see *Israel.*

MEGHALAYA: one of the twenty-one states of *India*, Meghalaya was part of *Assam* until it became a separate state in 1972.

MELAKA: alternative name is *Malacca*, part of *Malaysia.*

MELANESIA: composed of *New Caledonia, Solomon Islands*, the *Bismarck Archipelago, Fiji, Vanuatu,* and sometimes *New Guinea.*

MELILLA: enclave in *Morocco* belonging to *Spain.*

MELVILLE (Island): one of the *Parry Islands*, part of *Canada.*

MELVILLE (Island): part of *Australia*, (Northern Territory).

MENORCA (Island): alternative name is *Minorca*. One of the *Balearic Islands*, part of *Spain*.

MERRITT (Island): part of *USA*.

MESOPOTAMIA: former name of *Iraq*.

MEXIANA (Island): part of *Brazil*.

MEXICO: full name is *Estados Unidos Mexicanos*; former name is *New Spain*. The viceroyalty of New Spain was set up in 1535 under Spanish control. Spain eventually accepted Mexican independence in September 1821, and this was followed by several governments and dictatorships until foreign intervention was sought. The French had a brief empire in Mexico from 1864 to 1867. Another dictatorship followed from 1876 to 1911. After further years of civil strife, a democratic leader was elected in 1934 and much social reform took place. Islands under Mexican administration are *Tiburon, Cozumel, Angel de la Guarda, Revilla Gigedo Islands* and *Tres Marias Islands*.

MICHIGAN: the 26th state to join the federal republic of the *USA* in 1837, Michigan had been made part of the Northwest Territory in 1787. It passed from British to US control in 1812.

MICRONESIA: composed of the *Pacific Islands (USA), Guam, Nauru* and *Kiribati*.

MIDDLE ANDAMAN (Island): one of the *Andaman* Islands, part of *India*.

MIDDLE CAIOS (Island): alternative name for *Grand Caicos*, part of *Turks and Caicos Islands*.

MIDDLE CONGO: former name of *Congo*.

MIDDLE EAST: in modern usage the term has come to be applied to the lands around the Southern and Eastern shores of the Mediterranean Sea, ie from Morocco to the Arabian Peninsula, Iran and sometimes beyond. Formerly the central part was called the *Near East* as it applied to the region nearest to Europe. The wider term, Middle East, evolved during World War II when the term Middle East was given to the British Military Command in Egypt. Modern usage has enlarged the area included in the term to encompass the Muslim Arab World.

MIDWAY ISLANDS: the area was discovered by the *USA* in 1859, and formally annexed in 1867. The islands became a US naval base in World War II and are now administered by the US Department of the Interior. The group comprises *Sand* and the Eastern islands.

MILNE LAND (Island): part of *Greenland*.

MINDANAO (Island): part of the *Philippines*.

MINDORO (Island): part of the *Philippines*.

MINNESOTA: under British control from 1763 to 1783, the eastern section then became part of Northwest Territory and the western section became part of the territory acquired by the Louisiana Purchase of 1803. In 1858 it became the 32nd member state of the *USA*.

MINORCA (Island): alternative name is *Menorca*. One of the *Balearic Islands*, part of *Spain*.

MISOOL (Island): in *West Irian*, part of *Indonesia*.

MISSISSIPPI: part of *Louisiana* until 1763, eastern Mississippi then passed from French to British hands. In 1783 most of the area of modern Mississippi was ceded to the *USA*, and it became Mississippi Territory in 1789. In 1817 it became the 20th state to join the Union.

MISSOURI: held originally by Spain and then by France, Missouri was incorporated into the *USA* in the Louisiana Purchase of 1803. It became Missouri Territory in 1812 and achieved statehood as the 24th member state of the USA in 1821.

MIZORAM: formerly part of *Assam*, Mizoram became one of the nine union territories of *India* in 1972.

MOCAMBIQUE: alternative name for *Mozambique*.

MOENA: former name of *Muna*, part of *Indonesia*.

MOHELI (Island): part of the *Comoro Islands*.

MOLDAVIA: formerly known, with *Wallachia*, as the Danubian Principalities, these two regions of the Danube now make up most of *Rumania*. Under Turkish influence from the 15th century, they finally achieved independence as a union in 1861-62, adopting the name of Rumania. See also *Moldavian Soviet Socialist Republic*.

MOLDAVIAN SOVIET SOCIALIST REPUBLIC: one of the fifteen Soviet Socialist Republics. Eastern Moldavia was passed to Russia in 1791 and further territory was acquired in 1793 and 1812, notably Bessarabia. In 1924 the *USSR* established a Moldavian Autonomous Republic within the Ukraine. In 1940 a reduced Moldavian ASSR became a constituent republic of the USSR. See also *Moldavia*.

MOLOKAI (Island): one of the *Hawaiian Islands*, part of *USA*.

MOLUCCAS GROUP: alternative name is *Spice Islands*. Northern islands are Morotai, *Halmahera, Ternate, Tidore, Bacan* and Makian, with the groups of *Obi Islands* and *Sula Islands*; southern islands are *Buru, Ceram, Amboina, Wetar,* Kisar and the groups of *Tanimbar,* Banda, *Kai, Aru* and Babar, part of *Indonesia*.

MONACO: the area fell under Spanish protection from 1542 to 1641 and under French protection from 1641 to 1793 when it was annexed to France. The Sardinians protectd it from 1815 to 1861, when it again fell to the French as an independent state. A prince was proclaimed absolute ruler, until the first constituion was promulgated in 1911. It has been an independent principality since that time.

MONGOLIA: full names are *Mongolian People's Republic* or *Bûgd Nairamdah Mongol Ard Uls*. Mongolia is split into two areas: *Outer Mongolia*, which is the Mongolian People's Republic and an independent country; and *Inner Mongolia* which is the Inner Mongolian autonomous region of China, and has been part of Manchuria since 1949. Outer Mongolia was proclaimed an independent state in July 1921.

MONGOLIAN PEOPLE'S REPUBLIC: see *Mongolia*.

MONTANA: acquired by the *USA* from France in the Louisiana Purchase of 1803. It became Montana Territory in 1864 and in 1889 the 41st state to join the Union.

MONTENEGRO: one of the six constituent republics of *Yugoslavia* since 1946. A principality since the 14th century, Montenegro was twice occupied by the Turks. It became a kingdom in 1910 but was overrun in World War I and after union with *Serbia* in 1918 was absorbed into Yugoslavia.

MONTREAL (Island): part of *Canada*, (Ontario).

MONTSERRAT (Island): one of the *Leeward Islands*. The island was discovered in 1493 by Columbus and colonized by the British in 1632. France held the administration of Montserrat several times, but it was finally awarded to Britain in 1783, and remains a British crown colony.

MOOREA (Island): former name is *Eimeo*. One of the *Society Islands*, pat of *French Polynesia*.

MORATA (Island): former name of *Goodenough*. One of the *D'entrecasteaux Islands*, part of *Papua New Guina*.

MORESBY (Island): one of the *Queen Charlotte Islands*, part of *Canada*.

MORETON (Island): off the southeast coast of Queensland, part of *Australia*.

MOROCCO: former names are *Marrocco, Spanish Morocco* and *French Morocco*; full name is *Al-Mamlaka al-Maghrebia*. In the 19th century European countries tried to gain control of this strategically situated country. In 1912 the ruling Sultan agreed to a French protectorate of nearly nine-tenths of the area, with Spain administering a small southern area. On 2 March 1956 France and Spain relinquished their rights over

67

the country and it became independent. *Ifni*, a Spanish enclave in French Morocco, is now part of independent Morocco. Rio de Oro province of *Western Sahara* has been annexed by Morocco since Mauritania withdrew.

MOROTAI (Island): one of the *Moluccas Group*, part of *Indonesia*.

MORS (Island): part of *Denmark*.

MOUNT DESERT (Island): part of *USA*, (Maine).

MOZAMBIQUE: alternative name is *Mocambique*; former name is *Portuguese East Africa*; full name is the *People's Republic of Mozambique*. In 1505 a Portuguese settlement was established, and large estates were controlled. Mozambique was ruled as part of *Goa* in India by Portugal until 1752; thereafter it was given its own administration. This self rule was changed to colony status in 1910. Internal strife increased and the government was overthrown in 1974. On 25 June 1975 the area became independent.

MUANG THAI: see *Thailand*.

MULL (Island): one of the *Inner Hebrides*, off the coast of *Scotland*, part of *UK*.

MUNA (Island): former name is *Moena*, part of *Indonesia*.

MURUA (Island): alternative name for *Woodlark*, part of *Papua New Guinea*.

MUSCAT AND OMAN: former name of *Oman*.

MYTILENE (Island): alternative name for *Lesbos*; another alternative name is *Lesvos*. Part of *Greece*.

N

NAGALAND: one of the twenty-one states of *India*, Nagaland was part of *Assam* until it became a separate state in 1961.

NAGAR HAVELI: Portuguese enclave in *India*. It was given to India on 17 August 1961.

NAMIBIA: alternative name is *South West Africa*, former name is *German South West Africa*. In 1884 the German government proclaimed a protectorate over Lüderitz, and the rest of the area (South West Africa) was soon added. In 1920 *South Africa* began to administer South West Africa as a mandate. This mandate was withdrawn by the UN in 1966 and declared illegal by international court in 1971. The name Namibia was adopted for the area by the UN in 1969. Under the aegis of the UN negotiations for independence were still underway in 1980.

NANTUCKET (Island): part of *USA*, (Massachusetts).

NAOERO (Island): alternative name for *Nauru*.

NARBOROUGH (Island): alternative name for *Fernandina*. One of the *Galapagos Islands*, part of *Ecuador*.

NARODNA REPUBLIKA BULGARIA: see *Bulgaria*.

NATAL REPUBLIC: former name of part of *South Africa*. It was taken by the British in 1843 and in 1910 became a province of the *Union of South Africa*.

NATIONALIST CHINA: former unofficial name of *Taiwan*.

NAURU (Island): alternative name is *Naoero*, former name was *Pleasant Island*. It was discovered in 1798 by the British and annexed in 1888 by Germany. In 1920 it was placed under UN mandate to Australia. It gained independence on 1 February 1968.

NAVARINO (Island): in *Tierra del Fuego*, part of *Chile*.

NAVIGATORS (Islands): former name of *Western Samoa*.

NAXOS (Island): one of the *Cyclades Islands*, part of *Greece*.

NEAR EAST: a name formerly given to the countries nearest to Europe extending from the Mediterranean Sea to the Persian Gulf. The wider term *Middle East* evolved during World War II when the term middle east was given to the British Military Command in Egypt.

NEAR ISLANDS: section of the *Aleutian Islands*, part of *USA*, composed of Agattu and Attu.

NEBRASKA: this area first came under Spanish colonial influence, then was sold by the French to the USA in the Louisiana Purchase of 1803. It became Nebraska Territory in 1861, and in 1864 was the 36th state to join the Union.

NEDERLAND: alternative name for *Netherlands*.

NEDERLANDSE ANTILLEN: see *Netherlands Antilles*.

NEGRI SEMBILAN: one of the eleven federated states of *West Malaysia* on the Malay peninsula, it was formed in the 16th century from the settlements of the Minangkabaus from *Sumatra*. Coming under British influence after the Straits Settlements were founded in 1826, it was to accept a British Adviser (as Sungei Ujong) and as Negri Sembilan joined the Federated States of Malaya with *Perak, Pahang* and *Selangor* in 1896. It became a member state of the Malayan Union after World War II, the Federation of *Malaya* in 1948, and the Federation of Malaysia in 1963.

NEGROS (Island): one of the *Visayan Islands*, part of the *Philippines*.

NEJD: this region of central Arabia was captured from the Turks in 1913 by the Wahhabi leader Ibn Saud, who then incorporated the Asir region into it and personally united Nejd with the *Hijaz* to form the kingdom of *Saudi Arabia* on 20 September 1932.

NELSON (Island): part of *USA*, (Alaska).

NEPAL: in 1792 Nepal first entered into treaty with Britain. Gurkha wars led to a reduction of its boundaries. In 1923 Britain recognised Nepal's full sovereignty. Former name is *Nepaul*.

NEPAUL: former name of *Nepal*.

NETHERLANDS: alternative names are *Holland, Nederland*; full name is *Koninkrijk der Nederlanden*. The Union of Utrecht declared independence in 1581. Conflict with Spain from 1618 to 1648 resulted in the independence of the United provinces called Netherlands. The French overran the Netherlands from 1794 to 1795 and set up a kingdom under French protection. The area was invaded again during World War II when Germany took occupation. The country has remained a monarchy since the German collapse in 1945.

NETHERLANDS ANTILLES: alternative names are *Dutch Antilles* and *Dutch West Indies*, former name prior to 1949 is *Curaçao Territory*. Full name is *Nederlandse Antillen*. The area is composed of *Curaçao, Bonaire* and *Aruba* as well as the *Leeward Islands* of *Saba, St Eustatius* and the southern half of *St Martin*. The Netherlands Antilles have equal status with Holland in the Kingdom of the Netherlands.

NETHERLANDS EAST INDIES: former name of *Indonesia*.

NETHERLANDS GUIANA: former name of *Surinam*.

NETHERLANDS NEW GUINEA: former name of *Irian Jaya*, part of *Indonesia*.

NEUHANNOVER (Island): former name of *New Hanover*, part of *Papua New Guinea*.

NEUMECKLENBURG (Island): former name of *New Ireland*, in the *Bismarck Archipelago*, part of *Papua New Guinea*.

NEUPOMMERN (Island): former name of *New Britain*, in the *Bismarck Archipelago*, part of *Papua New Guinea*.

NEVADA: the area was settled by the Spanish but acquired by the United States from Mexico in the Mexican War. It was included into the region of Utah in 1850 and Congress made Nevada into a territory in 1861 to become the 36th state of the Union in 1864.

NEVIS (Island): part of *St Kitts-Nevis*.

NEW BRITAIN (Island): former name is *Neupommern*, in the *Bismarck Archipelago*, part of *Papua New Guinea*.

NEW BRUNSWICK: one of the twelve constituent provinces of *Canada*, it came under British control during the 18th century and became a colony in 1784. New Brunswick joined the other provinces in the dominion of Canada in 1867.

NEW CALEDONIA (Islands): alternative name is *Nouvelle-Calédonie*. Composed of *Loyalty Islands*, Huon Islands, Chesterfield Islands and Belep Islands. The islands were discovered in 1774 by Cook and claimed by France in 1853. They became a French overseas territory in 1946.

NEWFOUNDLAND AND LABRADOR: one of the twelve constituent provinces of *Canada*, the two territories were awarded to Britain by the French in 1763. Possession of Labrador was the subject of dispute between *Quebec* and Newfoundland at the beginning of this century, but eventually Newfoundland and Labrador became the 10th province of Canada in 1949.

NEW GEORGIA (Island): part of the *Solomon Islands*.

NEW GRANADA: former Spanish colony, in the 18th and 19th century. New Granada was a viceroyalty from 171 to 1739, and included *Colombia, Panama, Venezuela* and *Ecuador*. In 1830 Venezuela and Ecuador became separate states. Panama became a part of independent Colombia in 1821 and a separate state in 1903.

NEW GUINEA (Island): the *West Irian* section of the island is part of *Indonesia*, and the eastern section of the island is the main part of *Papua New Guinea*.

NEW GUINEA (Territory): part of *Papua New Guinea*; the northeast section which was mandated to Australia by the League of Nations in 1920.

NEW HAMPSHIRE: an English colony from 1679, New Hampshire was one of the Thirteen Colonies held by Britain and the first to declare independence in 1776. It became the 9th member state of the *USA* in 1788.

NEW HANOVER (Island): alternative name is *Lavongai*, former name is *Neuhannover*, part of *Papua New Guinea*.

NEW HEBRIDES (Islands): see *Vanuatu*.

NEW IRELAND (Island): former name is *Neumecklenburg*, in the *Bismarck Archipelago*, part of *Papua New Guinea*.

NEW JERSEY: New Jersey became a crown colony of the English in 1702. Of major importance during the American Revolution, in 1787 it became the 3rd state to ratify the Constitution and thus become a member state of the *USA*.

NEW MEXICO: founded as a Spanish colony in 1598, the territory was fought over by Indians and Spaniards throughout the following century. New Mexico became a province of *Mexico* on achieving independence from Spain in 1821 and after the Mexican War was ceded to the *USA* in 1848. It became New Mexico Territory in 1850 and the 47th state to join the Union in 1912.

NEW PHILIPPINES (Islands): former name of *Caroline Islands*, part of *Pacific Islands (USA)*.

NEW PROVIDENCE (Island): part of the *Bahamas*.

NEW SIBERIA (Island): alternative name for *Novaya Sibir*, part of *USSR*.

NEW SIBERIAN ISLANDS: composed of *Kotelnyy, Faddei, Novaya Sibir* and *Lyakhovskiy*, part of *USSR*.

NEW SOUTH WALES: one of the constituent states and territories of *Australia*, New South Wales was first colonized by the British in 1788. It became a federated state of Australia in 1901.

NEW SPAIN: former name of *Mexico*.

NEW YORK: the English won the New York area from the Dutch in 1667 and it remained one of the Thirteen Colonies held by the British until the American Revolution. New York ratified the Constitution of the *USA* in 1788 and became its 11th member state. It was for a short period (1789-90) the capital city of the federal republic.

NEW ZEALAND: it was discovered in 1642 by Tasman, the first missionaies arrived in 1814 and in 1840 the first settlement was established under the dependency of New South Wales. The following year, 1841, New Zealand became a separate British colony. Self-government was achieved in 1852. The dominion consists of *North Island, South Island, Stewart Island* and *Chatham Islands*. Other islands belonging to New Zealand are: *Auckland, Campbell, Antipodes,* Three Kings, *Bounty,* Snares, and Solander. Islands which are dependencies of New Zealand are: *Kermadec Islands, Cook, Tokelau, Niue* and *Ross Dependency.*

NIAS (Island): part of *Indonesia.*

NICARAGUA: full name is *República de Nicaragua*. Under Spanish rule, Nicaragua was part of the administration of *Guatemala*. The area declared independence from Spain in 1821 and was a member of the *Central American Federation* from 1825 to 1838. The US marines landed in Nicaragua in 1912 to assist in quelling civil strife, and were only withdrawn in 1933. Now an independent republic.

NICOBAR ISLANDS: composed of *Great Nicobar*, Teressa and Camorta, part of *India.*

NIGER: full name *République du Niger*. In 1885 the territory came under French influence, and in 1900 it became a military territory within upper Senegal-Niger. This passed to *French West Africa* in 1922. The area became a republic on 18 December 1958 and achieved full independence on 3 August 1960.

NIGERIA: full name is *Federal Republic of Nigeria*. The British arrived in the area in the 19th century as traders and explorers, and soon established their rule in the south-western parts. By 1906 Britain controlled the whole area and the colony was established in 1914. Independence was gained on 1 October 1960. In 1961 the northern part of *British Cameroon* was joined to Nigeria and the Republic of Nigeria was proclaimed on 1 October 1963. In the eastern region of Nigeria fighting broke out and the Republic of *Biafra* was proclaimed on 30 May 1967. The war lasted until 15 January 1970 when Biafra rejoined Nigeria. Nigeria is a federation of the following nineteen states: Anambra, Banchi, Bendel, Benue, Borno, Cross River, Gongola, Imo, Kaduna, Kano, Kwara, Lagos, Niger, Ogun, Ondo, Oyo, Plateau, Rivers and Sokoto.

NIHON: an alternative name for *Japan.*

NIIHAU (Island): one of the *Hawaiian* Islands, part of *USA.*

NIKUMARORO (Island): former name is *Gardner* Island, one of the *Phoenix Islands*, part of *Kiribati.*

NIPPON: an alternative name for *Japan.*

NIUE (Island): former name is *Savage* Island. Originally part of the Cook Island administration but separate since 1922. Discovered in 1774 by Captain Cook. A dependency of *New Zealand*.

NORDAUSTLANDET (Island): alternative name for *North East Land*, part of *Svalbard*.

NORFOLK (Island): it was discovered in 1774 by Cook and made into a prison Island from 1788 to 1855. The island was annexed to *Tasmania* in 1844, then became a dependency of *New South Wales* in 1896. This settlement was transferred to *Australia* in 1913.

NORGE: alternative name for *Norway*.

NORMANBY (Island): one of the *D'entrecasteaux Islands*, part of *Papua New Guinea*.

NORMAN ISLES: former name for *Channel Islands*, part of *UK*.

NORTH ANDAMAN (Island): one of the *Andaman Islands*, part of *India*.

NORTH BORNEO: former name of *Sabah*, part of *Malaysia*.

NORTH CAROLINA: an English colony under proprietary rule from the mid-17th century, it was made a crown colony proper from 1729. In 1784 the western region was ceded to the *USA*, later forming *Tennessee*. In 1789 North Carolina became the 12th state to join the Union.

NORTH DAKOTA: the northwestern half of this area became part of the *USA* with the Louisiana Purchase of 1803, the southeastern half being ceded to the *USA* by Britain in 1818. In 1861 Dakota Territory was set up, covering the Dakotas North and South and some neighbouring lands. In 1889 the Dakotas were split into separate states and North Dakota became the 39th state to join the Union.

NORTH EAST LAND (Island): alternative name is *Nordaustlandet*, part of *Svalbard*, in Norway.

NORTH ISLAND: part of *New Zealand*.

NORTHERN IRELAND: Ireland was conquered by the Normans in 1169-71 and English rule was established around Dublin. It was Cromwell in the mid 17th century that subdued all Ireland. The United Kingdom of Great Britain and Ireland was formed in 1801. The Republic of Ireland was formed in 1922. Northern Ireland was established in 1920 and United Kingdom of Great Britain and Northern Ireland was formed in 1927.

NORTHERN RHODESIA: former name of *Zambia*.

NORTHERN TERRITORY: one of the two territories and six states which constitute the Commonwealth of *Australia*. First permanently settled in 1869, Northern Territory was part of *New South Wales* from 1825 to 1863 and of *South Australia* from 1863 to 1911, when it joined the Commonwealth of Australia.

NORTH KOREA: full name is *Chosun Minchu-chui Inmin Konghwhaguk*. Part of *Korea* until its partition after World War II into Russian and American occupied zones. The Russians established a provisional communist government in North Korea soon after their arrival in 1945. On 9 September 1948 it was proclaimed the *People's Democratic Republic of Korea*.

NORTH UIST (Island): one of the *Outer Hebrides*, off the coast of *Scotland*, part of the *UK*.

NORTH VIETNAM: former name of northern *Vietnam*. North Vietnam was the name used from 1954 to 1976. The name Vietnam was in use between 1945 and 1954 and after 1976.

NORTHWEST TERRITORIES: one of the twelve provinces of the Canadian federation known as a 'territory', it occupies a large part of modern *Canada*. The Northwest Territories were sold by the Hudson's Bay Company to the Canadian confederation in 1870. The present boundaries were resolved in 1912.

NORTH YEMEN: former name of *Yemen Arab Republic*.

NORWAY: alternative name is *Norge*; full name is *Kongeriket Norge*. The area was ruled by *Denmark* until 1814 when it was ceded to *Sweden*. Norway was an independent kingdom in union with Sweden until 1905, when Norway became an independent monarchy. Islands included in Norway are *Senja, Hinn, Svalbard, Jan Mayen, Bouvet, Lofoten* and Vesterålen.

NOUVELLE-CALEDONIE (Island): alternative name for *New Caledonia*.

NOUVELLES HEBRIDES: see *Vanuatu*.

NOVA SCOTIA: an island region which is one of the twelve constituent provinces of *Canada*. Conceded by France to Britain in 1763, it became a colony separate from *Prince Edward Island* and Cape Breton by 1784. It acceded to the Canadian confederation as one of the four original members in 1867.

NOVAYA SIBIR (Island): alternative name is *New Siberia*, one of the *New Siberian Islands*, part of *USSR*.

NOVAYA ZEMLYA, North Island: part of *USSR*.

NOVAYA ZEMLYA, South Island: part of *USSR*.

NUBIA: see *Sudan*.

NUKU HIVA (Island): one of the *Marquesas Islands*, part of *French Polynesia*.

NUNIVAK (Island): part of *USA*, (Alaska).

NYASALAND: former name of *Malawi*.

O

OAHU (Island): one of the *Hawaiian* Islands, part of *USA*.

OBI ISLANDS: composed of Obiro, Bisa, Obi Latu and Tobalai islands, within the *Moluccas Group*, part of *Indonesia*.

OBIRA (Island): one of the *Obi Islands*, within the *Moluccas Group*, part of *Indonesia*.

OCEAN (Island): has reverted back to its pre-colonial name of *Banaba* Island, part of *Kiribati*.

OCEANIA: composed of *Micronesia, Polynesia* and *Melanesia*.

OGASAWARA-GUNTO (Islands): alternative name for *Bonin* islands. These islands were handed back to Japan by the USA on 26 June 1968, now part of *Japan*.

OHIO: bounded by Lake Erie on the north, Ohio was an early attraction for fur traders, with the land contested by Indians, French and British. In 1774 Britain incorporated the area into *Canada*, but ceded it to the *USA* in 1783 after the American Revolution. Ohio became a territory in 1799 and achieved statehood in 1803; the 17th to join the Union.

OKINAWA (Islands): a group in the *Ryukyu Islands*. Returned to Japan by the USA in 1972, part of *Japan*.

OKLAHOMA: acquired by the *USA* in the Louisiana Purchase of 1803, the history of the area was dominated by its Indian tribes until white settlements began in earnest in the 1880s. The western section became Oklahoma Territory in 1890, including the 'Texas Panhandle' strip of territory. Indian Territory and Oklahoma Territory were joined in 1907 to form the state of Oklahoma, the 46th member state of the USA.

OKTYABRSKOY REVOLYUTSH (Island): one of the *Severnaya Zemlya Islands*, part of *USSR*.

ÖLAND (Island): part of *Sweden*.

OMAN: full name is *Saltanat Oman*; former names are *Muscat and Oman* and Masqat wah Oman. Oman is a sultanate which in the 19th century, was the most powerful state in *Arabia*. In 1970 the name changed from Muscat and Oman to the present form. The *Kuria Muria* Islands are part of Oman.

OMBAI (Island): alternative name for *Alor*, one of the *Lesser Sunda Islands*, part of *Indonesia*.

ONTARIO: one of the twelve constituent provinces of *Canada*, it was conceded by France to Britain in 1763. It was repeatedly joined to and separated from *Quebec* until both became separate provinces on joining the Canadian confederation in 1867.

ONTONG JAVA ISLANDS: former name is *Lord Howe* Islands, part of the *Solomon Islands*.

ORANGE FREE STATE REPUBLIC: former name of part of *South Africa*. Prior to 1848 the Orange Free State area was not an official district. In 1848 the area was proclaimed the *Orange River Souvereignty* under British Rule. In 1854 the Orange Free State Republic was established under Boer rule. In 1900 Britain annexed the territory and it became known as the *Orange River Colony*. In 1910 it became a province of the *Union of South Africa*.

ORANGE RIVER COLONY: former name of part of *South Africa*. Other former names of this area are *Orange Free State Republic* and *Orange River Sovereignty*. In 1910 it became a province of the *Union of South Africa*.

ORANGE RIVER SOVEREIGNTY: former name of part of *South Africa*. Other former names of this area are *Orange River Colony* and *Orange Free State Republic*. In 1910 it became a province of the *Union of South Africa*.

OREGON: the first settlement in Oregon was founded by the Pacific Fur Company of the Astor family in the early 19th century. In 1818 joint rights to the Oregon region were assigned to Britain and the USA. Oregon Territory was created in 1848, being later reduced to admit Washington Territory, and in 1859 Oregon became the 33rd state to join the Union.

ORISSA: one of the twenty-one states of *India*, the region was conquered by the British in 1803. In 1936 the province of Orissa was formed and in 1948-9 it was enlarged to incorporate twenty-four former principalities. Orissa became a member state of the *Union of India* in 1950.

ORKNEY ISLANDS: off the coast of *Scotland*, part of the *UK*. Orkney and Shetland Islands were originally ruled by Norway, the islands were pledged to James III of Scotland as security for the dowry of Margaret, James's Queen, in 1468. The pledge was not redeemed and the islands were annexed to Scotland in 1472. Composed of *Pomona* (Mainland), South Ronaldsay, Westray, Sanday, Stronsay and Hoy.

ORLEANS (Ile d'): part of *Canada*, (Quebec).

ORONA (Island): former name is *Hull* Island, one of the *Phoenix Islands*, part of *Kiribati*.

OSEL (Island): former name of *Sarema*, part of *USSR*.

OSTERREICH: alternative name for *Austria*.

OSTERO (Island): part of the *Faroe Islands*.

OTTOMAN EMPIRE: former name of an area including present-day *Turkey*, *Rumania*, *Bulgaria*, *Albania* and *Yugoslavia*. This vast state existed from the late 13th century until its dissolution in 1918. The area covered varied from time to time, with Turkey as the main centre of the Ottoman Empire.

OUTER HEBRIDES (Islands): off the coast of *Scotland*, part of the *UK*. The group is composed of *Lewis with Harris, North Uist, South Uist, Barra*, and smaller islands.

OUTER MONGOLIA: see *Mongolia*.

P

PACIFIC ISLANDS (USA): composed of Marianas Islands (excluding Guam and the Northern Marianas), Caroline Islands (excluding Belau) and the Marshall Islands. All the islands of these groups were acquired by Germany (except Guam) but seized by Japan in 1914. During World War II the islands were occupied by the US forces and in 1947 the UN approved the US trusteeship of the area. On 12 July 1978 the *Caroline Islands* (except Belau) approved a constitution for a Federated States of Micronesia. (Belau became a Republic on 1 January 1981.) On 10 November 1980 the Marshall Islands and Micronesia agreed on future self government as the Federated States of Micronesia in free association with the USA. This is still to be approved by the USA and the UN before the termination of the 1947 trusteeship. Northern Marianas fall under a covenant made on 24 March 1976 to establish a Commonwealth of the Northern Marianas Islands which will become fully effective on termination of the US trusteeship agreement.

PACIFIC ISLAND TRUST TERRITORY: full name of *Pacific Islands (USA)*.

PADRE (Island): part of *USA*, (Texas).

PAG (Island): former name is *Pago*, part of *Yugoslavia*.

PAGO (Island): former name of *Pag*, part of *Yugoslavia*.

PAHANG: one of the eleven federated states of *West Malaysia* on the Malay peninsula, it came under British control in 1888 and in 1896 formed with *Selangor, Negri Sembilan* and *Perak* the Federated Malay States. After World War II it became a member state of the Malayan Union, the Federation of *Malaya* in 1948 and the Federation of Malaysia in 1963.

PAKISTAN: full name is *Islamic Republic of Pakistan*; former name is *West Pakistan*. The area was overrun by Afghans in the late 18th century. The British attempted to subdue the area in the Afghan wars of the 19th century. The Moslem League wanted a Moslem State and Britain agreed to the formation of Pakistan as a separate dominion from India on 15 August 1947. The Hindu-dominated *Jammu-Kashmir* became signed to India in October 1947, but Pakistan fought for the area unsuccessfully. The smaller part of *Kashmir*, known as Azad Kashmir, is controlled by Pakistan. Pakistan became an Islamic Republic in 1956, a year after East and West Pakistan had been so named. Both halves of Pakistan were one republic within the Commonwealth from 1955 to 1971. East Pakistan became independent *Bangladesh* on 26 December 1971.

PALAU ISLANDS: former name of *Belau*, within the *Caroline Islands*, gained independence as the Republic of *Belau* on 1 January 1981.

PALAWAN (Islands): former name is *Paragua*, part of the *Philippines*.

PALESTINE: former name of *Israel*. Overrun successively by the Romans, Persians, Moslem Arabs, Christian crusaders, Mamelukes, and Ottoman Turks, Palestine began to be settled by the Jews in the 19th century. After World War I Britain was granted a League of Nations mandate for Palestine (1922). The Palestine question was passed to the UN in 1947. The area was proclaimed the *State of Israel* in 1948.

PANAMA: full name is *Republica de Panama*. The area was subordinated to the Spanish viceroyalty of *Peru* until 1717 when it became part of the viceroyalty of *New Granada* with modern *Colombia, Ecuador* and *Venezuela*. In 1739 Ecuador and Venezuela left the viceroyalty. In 1830 Panama joined Colombia in the Republic of New Granada until 1858. Panama was established as a new republic at the time when the *Panama Canal Zone* became an important question; in 1903 the area was proclaimed a republic with USA support. The Ilha de *Coiba*, and *Pearle Islands* are part of Panama.

PANAMA CANAL ZONE: the canal was built by the *USA* between 1904 and 1914, on territory leased from *Panama*. In 1977 a new agreement was reached, replacing the original 1903 document and stating that by the year 2000 the canal would revert to Panamanian control with the USA retaining rights to defend the canal's neutrality. Alternative name is *Canal Zone*.

PANAY (Island): one of the *Visayan Islands*, part of the *Philippines*.

PAPA STOUR (Island): one of the *Shetland Islands*, in *Scotland*, part of the *UK*.

PAPUA NEW GUINEA: formerly two sections of Papua and *New Guinea*, comprising the eastern half of the whole island of *New Guinea*. Papua was annexed by Queensland in 1883 and became British New Guinea. This area passed to Australia in 1905 as the Territory of Papua. The northern part was German New Guinea from 1884 to 1914 and became mandated to Australia in 1920 after which it became known as the Territory of New Guinea. In 1949 the territories of Papua and New Guinea were merged administratively. On 1 December 1973, they became the self-governing country of Papua New Guinea. Full independence was gained on 16 September 1975. Islands included in the area are: *Woodlark, Buka, Manus, New Hanover* and *Bougainville*; island groups included are: *Bismarck Archipelago, D'entrecasteaux Islands, Louisiade Archipelago* and *Trobriand Islands*.

PARAGUA (Island): former name of *Palawan*, part of the *Philippines*.

PARAGUAY: full name is *República del Paraguay*. Spanish influence came to the area from 1516, and real independence was only asserted in 1721. In 1776 the area again became a viceroyalty of the Rio de la Plata under Spain. From 1814 a series of dictators ruled until the war with Brazil (1865). Many different governments have held power until present times. It is an independent republic governed under the 1967 constitution.

PARAMUSHIR (Island): one of the *Kuril Islands*, part of the *USSR*.

PARRY ISLANDS: composed of *Melville, Bathurst, Devon, Prince Patrick, Cornwallis* and many smaller islands, part of *Canada*.

PASCUA (Island): official name of *Easter Island*, part of *Chile*.

PEARLE ISLANDS: the Spanish name is Archipiélago de las Perlas. Principal islands are San Miguel, San José, Pedro González, Saboga, part of *Panama*.

PELENG (Island): in the *Banggai Archipelago*, part of *Indonesia*.

PEMBA (Island): part of *Tanzania*.

PENANG (Island): alternative name is *Pinang*, part of *Malaysia*.

PENINSULAR MALAYSIA: former name is *Malaya*, part of *Malaysia*.

PENNSYLVANIA: settled in the 17th century by the English, Dutch and Swedes, Pennsylvania came under the proprietory control of English Quakers. In 1776 it was created a state and in 1787 Pennsylvania became the 2nd state to ratify the Constitution of the new confederation of the *USA*.

PEOPLE'S DEMOCRATIC REPUBLIC OF KOREA: see *North Korea*.

PEOPLE'S DEMOCRATIC REPUBLIC OF YEMEN: see *Yemen*.

PEOPLE'S REPUBLIC OF BANGLADESH: see *Bangladesh*.

PEOPLE'S REPUBLIC OF BENIN: see *Benin*.

PEOPLE'S REPUBLIC OF CHINA: see *China*.

PEOPLE'S REPUBLIC OF THE CONGO: see *Congo*.

PEOPLE'S REPUBLIC OF MOZAMBIQUE: see *Mozambique*.

PERAK: one of the eleven federated states of *West Malaysia* on the Malay peninsula, Perak was second only in importance to *Johore* in the trading days of the 17th century. It came under British influence after the founding of the Straits Settlements in 1826 and in 1896 joined *Pahang, Selangor* and *Negri Sembilan* to form the Federated Malay States. After World War II Perak became a member state of the

Malayan Union, then the Federation of *Malaya* in 1948 and the Federation of Malaysia in 1963.

PERIM (Island): island in the entrance to the Red Sea, part of *Yemen*.

PERLIS: one of the eleven federated states of *West Malaysia* on the Malay peninsula, Perlis was one of the four northern kingdoms which fell under Siamese influence from the 16th century. Under the Anglo-Siamese Treaty of 1826 it remained under Siamese control but was regained by Britain in 1909. With *Kedah*, *Kelantan* and *Terengganu* (and *Johore*) it became part of the Unfederated Malay States. After World War II Perlis became a member state of the Malayan Union, then the Federation of *Malaya* in 1948 and the Federation of Malaysia in 1963.

PERSIA: former name of *Iran*.

PERU: full name is *República del Peru*. In the late 16th century the viceroyalty of Peru was expanded to include most of Spanish ruled South America. In the 18th century with the formation of *New Granada*, Peru's size was much reduced. Peru achieved independence in 1821, but this was only recognized by Spain in 1879, since when it has been a republic frequently under dictatorship. The constitution was suspended in 1968.

PHILIPPINES: full names are *Republic of the Philippines*, *República de Filipinas* and *Republika ñg Pilipinas*. The islands were named after the Spanish King Philip, and Spain had a strong foothold there by the mid-16th century. The Filipinos fought the Spanish and declared their independence in the late 19th century. In 1898 the Philippines were given to the USA by Spain after the Spanish-American war. The USA worked towards self-rule for the islands, but the growing aggression of Japan prevented this from reaching fruition. The commonwealth of the Philippines was finally established in 1935, but was occupied by the Japanese in World War II. Independence was achieved on 4 July 1946. Island groups in the Philippines are *Visayan Islands* and the *Sulu Archipelago*. Other individual islands are: *Basilan, Catanduanes, Mindoro, Palawan, Mindanao* and *Luzon*.

PHOENIX ISLANDS: composed of *Abariringa, Enderbury, Rawaki, Nikumaroro, Orona, Manra*, McKean and Birnie, part of *Kiribati*.

PHOENIX (Island): former name of *Rawaki* Island, (as distinct from the Phoenix Island Group whose name remains unchanged) one of the *Phoenix Islands*, part of *Kiribati*.

PICO (Island): one of the *Azores Islands*, part of *Portugal*.

PIGALU (Island): former name of *Annobón*, Isla de, part of *Equatorial Guinea*.

PILIPINAS: alternative name for the *Philippines*.

PINANG (Island): alternative name is *Penang*; one of the eleven federated states of *West Malaysia*, it was acquired by the British from the Sultan of Kedah in 1786. In 1826 it was merged with *Malacca* and *Singapore* to form the Straits Settlements. After World War II the Straits Settlements joined the Malayan Union, and Pinang subsequently became a member state of the Federation of *Malaya* in 1948 and the Federation of Malaysia in 1963.

PINES (Isle of): former name of Isle of *Youth*, part of *Cuba*.

PIRATE COAST: former name of *United Arab Emirates*.

PITCAIRN (Island): The British took possession of the island in 1839, although it had been settled by mutineers of the Bounty in 1790. The island is administered by the British High Commissioner in New Zealand. The other three islands in the group are Henderson, Oeno, Ducie.

PITT (Island): part of *Canada*, (British Columbia).

PITT (Island): off the coast of New Zealand, part of the *Chatham Islands*, belonging to *New Zealand*.

PLEASANT (Island): former name of *Nauru*.

POLAND: full name is *Polska Rzeczpospolita Ludowa*. After World War I Poland was able to regain its independence, on 9 November 1918. Germany invaded Poland in 1939 and precipitated World War II. A people's democracy was established in 1944 and former German territories along the line of the rivers Oder and Neisse came under Polish sovereignty. In 1947 a pro soviet government was elected.

POLSKA RZECZPOSPOLITA LUDOWA: see *Poland*.

POLYNESIA: composed of *French Polynesia, Niue, Cook Islands, Tokelau Islands, Tuvalu, Tonga Islands, Samoa Islands* and *Hawaii*.

POLYNESIE FRANCAISE: alternative name for *French Polynesia*.

POMONA (Island): alternative name is *Mainland Island*, one of the *Orkney Islands* in *Scotland*, part of the *UK*.

PONAPE (Island): one of the *Caroline Islands*, part of *Pacific Islands (USA)*.

PONDICHERRY: one of the nine union territories of *India*. It contains four former French enclaves which were formally handed over to India in 1962.

PORTO RICO: former name of *Puerto Rico*.

PORTUGAL: full name is *República Portuguesa*. The Portuguese Empire extended across the world in the 15th century, reaching a climax in the 16th century. The rise of Spain and France led to economic instability and the Portuguese royal family feld to Brazil. The French were driven out in 1811 and the Portuguese monarchy was overthrown in 1910. Slowly Portugal's overseas possessions dwindled to a few islands. Island groups controlled by Portugal are the *Madeira Islands* and the *Azores.*

PORTUGUESE EAST AFRICA: former name of *Mozambique.*

PORTUGUESE GUINEA: former name of *Guinea-Bissau.*

PORTUGUESE TIMOR: former name of *East Timor* which has joined with *West Timor* to become *Timor*, part of *Indonesia.*

PRADES THAI: see *Thailand.*

PRATHET THAI: see *Thailand.*

PRINCE CHARLES (Island): part of *Canada*, (Northwest Territory).

PRINCE EDWARD ISLAND: one of the twelve constituent provinces of *Canada*, it was annexed to *Nova Scotia* before becoming a separate British colony in 1769. The island joined the Canadian confederation in 1873.

PRINCE OF WALES (Island): part of *Canada.*

PRINCE OF WALES (Island): in the *Alexander Archipelago*, part of *USA.*

PRINCE PATRICK (Island): one of the *Parry Islands*, part of *Canada.*

PRINCESS ROYAL (Island): part of *Canada*, (British Columbia).

PRINCIPAT D'ANDORRA: see *Andorra.*

PRINCIPE (Island): part of *São Tome and Principe.*

PRUSSIA: formerly a German State. The provinces of East and West Prussia were united from 1824-1878. The German empire was founded under Prussian leadership in 1871 and became a Republic in 1918. After World War II the eastern part of Prussia went to Poland and the northern section to USSR. Prussia was formally abolished by the Allied Control Council on 1 March 1947.

PUERTO RICO: former name is *Porto Rico*. A settlement was founded on the island in 1521 and slaves were introduced for sugar plantations. Slavery was abolished in 1873 and greater self-government was granted by Spain to the Puerto Ricans in February 1898. A few months later, after the Spanish-American war, Puerto Rico was ceded to the USA. In 1946 the USA granted more autonomy to the island and by 25 July 1952 the Commonwealth of Puerto Rico was proclaimed. The name Porto Rico had changed to Puerto Rico in 1932. *Crab* Island is part of Puerto Rico.

PUNJAB: one of the twenty-one states of *India*, this historic area of civilization was annexed by the British in the mid-19th century. In 1947 part of the Punjab was allotted to *Pakistan*, the remainder becoming a state in the *Union of India*.

PYIDAUNGSU SOCIALIST THAMMADA MYANMA NAINGNGAN-DAW: see *Burma*.

Q

QATAR: full name is *State of Qatar*; alternative name is *Katar*. The sheikdom fell under British protection from 1916 to 1 September 1971 when it gained independence.

QESHM (Island): former name is *Kishm*, alternative name is *Qishm*, part of *Iran*.

QISHM (Island): alternative name is *Qeshm*, part of *Iran*.

QITA GHAZZAH: alternative name for the *Gaza Strip*, part of *Israel*.

QUEBEC: one of the twelve constituent provinces of *Canada*, perpetually in dispute between France and Britain, the area of Quebec was known as Lower Canada in the 18th century after the British detached Upper Canada (now *Ontario*) in 1791. Upper and Lower Canada were reunited in 1841 and in 1867 Quebec joined the new confederation of Canada as a separate province. French is the official language of Quebec.

QUEEN CHARLOTTE ISLANDS: off the coast of British Columbia, composed of *Graham* Island, *Moresby* Island and *Kunghit* Island, part of *Canada*.

QUEEN ELIZABETH ISLANDS: composed of *Axel-Heiberg* island, *Ellesmere* island and *Amund Ringnes* island, part of *Canada*.

QUEEN MAUD LAND: in the Norwegian part of *Antarctica*.

QUEENSLAND: one of the constituent states and territories of *Australia*, Queensland originally formed a part of *New South Wales*. The area was separated from New South Wales in 1859 to become a British colony. The state joined federated Australia in 1901.

QUELPART, SAISHU: former name of *Cheju*, part of *South Korea*.

QUITO: ancient name of *Ecuador*.

R

RAIATEA (Island): one of the *Society Islands*, part of *French Polynesia*.

RAJA AMPAT ISLANDS: composed of *Waigeo* island and smaller islands, in *West Irian*, part of *Indonesia*.

RAJASTHAN: one of the twenty-one states of *India*, Rajasthan was formed in 1948 from many of the former principalities of Rajputna.

RALIK CHAIN: chain of islands in the *Marshall Islands*. The most important are Jaluit, *Kwajalein*, Wotho and Eniwetok, part of *Pacific Islands (USA)*.

RAMREE (Island): alternative name for *Yanbye*, part of *Burma*.

RAMSEY (Island): in St George's Channel off the southwest coast of Wales. Part of Pembroke County, *Wales, UK*.

RAPA NUI: former name of *Easter Island*.

RAROTONGA (Island): formerly *Goodenough Island*, part of the *Cook Islands*.

RAS AL-KHAIMAH: one of the seven federated *United Arab Emirates*, Ras al-Khaimah was affiliated with *Sharjah* before becoming a separate sheikdom under British protection in 1921. It joined the UAE in 1972.

RATAK CHAIN: chain of islands in the *Marshall Islands*. The most important are Mili, Majuro, Maloelap, Wotje, Likiep, and Bikini, part of *Pacific Islands (USA)*.

RATHLIN (Island): in the North Channel off the northeast coast of Northern Ireland. Administered by County Antrim, *Northern Ireland, UK*.

RAT ISLANDS: within the *Aleutian Archipelago*. Composed of Semisopochnio, Amchitka and Kisa, part of the *USA*.

RAWAKI (Island): former name is *Phoenix* Island, (as distinct from the Phoenix Island group whose name remains unchanged), one of the *Phoenix Islands*, part of *Kiribati*.

REDONDA (Island): island in the *Leeward Islands*, West Indies, part of *Antigua and Barbuda*.

REINA ADELAIDA ARCHIPELAGO: group of islands off the southwest coast of *Chile* of which they are part.

REPUBBLICA ITALIANA: see *Italy*.

REPUBBLICA DI SAN MARINO: see *San Marino*.

REPUBLICA ARGENTINA: see *Argentina*.

REPUBLICA DE BOLIVIA: see *Bolivia.*
REPUBLICA DE CABO VERDE: see *Cape Verde Islands.*
REPUBLICA DE CHILE: see *Chile.*
REPUBLICA DE COLOMBIA: see *Colombia.*
REPUBLICA DE COSTA RICA: see *Costa Rica.*
REPUBLICA DE CUBA: see *Cuba.*
REPUBLICA DE EL SALVADOR: see *El Salvador.*
REPUBLICA DE FILIPINAS: see *Philippines.*
REPUBLICA DE GUATEMALA: see *Guatemala.*
REPUBLICA DE GUINEA ECUATORIAL: see *Equatorial Guinea.*
REPUBLICA DE HONDURAS: see *Honduras.*
REPUBLICA DEL ECUADOR: see *Ecuador.*
REPUBLICA DEL PARAGUAY: see *Paraguay.*
REPUBLICA DEL PERU: see *Peru.*
REPUBLICA DE NICARAGUA: see *Nicaragua.*
REPUBLICA DE PANAMA: see *Panama.*
REPUBLICA DE VENEZUELA: see *Venezuela.*
REPUBLICA DOMINICANA: see *Dominican Republic.*
REPUBLICA FEDERATIVA DO BRASIL: see *Brazil.*
REPUBLICA ORIENTAL DEL URUGUAY: see *Uruguay.*
REPUBLICA PORTUGUESA: see *Portugal.*
REPUBLICA SOCIALISTA ROMANIA: see *Rumania.*
REPUBLIC OF BELAU: see *Belau.*
REPUBLIC OF CHINA: see *Taiwan.*
REPUBLIC OF DJIBOUTI: see *Djibouti.*
REPUBLIC OF INDONESIA: see *Indonesia.*
REPUBLIC OF KOREA: see *South Korea.*
REPUBLIC OF SINGAPORE: see *Singapore.*
REPUBLIC OF SOUTH AFRICA: see *South Africa.*
REPUBLIC OF THE MALDIVES: see *Maldive Islands.*
REPUBLIC OF THE PHILIPPINES: see *Philippines.*

REPUBLIC OF TOGO: see *Togo*.
REPUBLIC OF ZAMBIA: see *Zambia*.
REPUBLIEK VAN SUID-AFRIKA: see *South Africa*.
REPUBLIKA NG PILIPINAS: see *Philippines*.
REPUBLIKA POPULLORE SOCIALISTE E SHQIPERERISE: see *Albania*.
REPUBLIKKA TA MALTA: see *Malta*.
REPUBLIKEN FINLAND: see *Finland*.
REPUBLIK INDONESIA: see *Indonesia*.
REPUBLIK OSTERREICH: see *Austria*.
REPUBLIQUE ALGERIENNE DEMOCRATIQUE ET POPULAIRE: see *Algeria*.
REPUBLIQUE DE COTE D'IVOIRE: see *Ivory Coast*.
REPUBLIQUE DE GUINEE: see *Guinea*.
REPUBLIQUE DE HAUTE-VOLTA: see *Upper Volta*.
REPUBLIQUE DE ZAIRE: see *Zaïre*.
REPUBLIQUE D'HAITI: see *Haiti*.
REPUBLIQUE DU MALI: see *Mali*.
REPUBLIQUE DU NIGER: see *Niger*.
REPUBLIQUE DU SENEGAL: see *Senegal*.
REPUBLIQUE DU TCHAD: see *Chad*.
REPUBLIQUE FRANCAISE: see *France*.
REPUBLIQUE GABONAISE: see *Gabon*.
REPUBLIQUE ISLAMIQUE DE MAURITANIE: see *Mauritania*.
REPUBLIQUE POPULAIRE DU BENIN: see *Benin*.
REPUBLIQUE POPULAIRE DU CONGO: see *Congo*.
REPUBLIQUE TOGOLAISE: see *Togo*.
REPUBLIQUE UNIE DU CAMEROUN: see *Cameroon*.
REUNION (Island): former name is *Bourbon*, one of the *Mascarene Islands*, part of *France* as an overseas department since 1947.
REVILLA GIGEDO ISLANDS: island group in the Pacific Ocean off the coast of Colima. Composed of *Socorro*, San Benedicto and *Clarión* Islands, part of *Mexico*.

REVILLAGIGEDO (Island): in the *Alexander Archipelago*, part of the *USA*.

RHODE ISLAND: full name is the State of Rhode Island and Providence Plantations. Settled by English Puritans in the 17th century, it became one of the Thirteen Colonies under British control. Although it won independence with the American Revolution, it did not join the new confederation of the *USA* until 1790, as its 13th member state.

RHODES (Island): alternative name is *Rodhos*, one of the *Dodecanese Islands*, part of *Greece*.

RHODESIA: former name of *Zimbabwe*.

RIESCO (Island): off the south Chile coast west of the Brunswick Peninsula, part of *Chile*.

RIO MUNI: the mainland part of *Equatorial Guinea*, sometimes known as Mbini which is the former name of the Rio Benito River.

RODHOS (Island): alternative name for *Rhodes*, one of the *Dodecanese Islands*, part of *Greece*.

RODRIQUES (Island): one of the *Mascarene Islands*, part of *Mauritius*.

ROMANIA: alternative name for *Rumania*.

ROSS DEPENDENCY: *New Zealand* dependency in *Antarctica*.

ROUMANIA: alternative for *Rumania*.

ROYALE (Isle): part of the *USA*, (Michigan).

ROYAUME DE BELGIQUE: see *Belgium*.

RUANDA: alternative name for *Rwanda*.

RUGEN (Island): part of the *German Democratic Republic*.

RUM (Island): alternative spelling is Isle of Rhum. One of the *Inner Hebrides*, off the coast of *Scotland*, part of the *UK*.

RUMANIA: full name is *Republica Socialista Romania*; alternative names are *Roumania* and *Romania*. The area fell under Ottoman rule in the 16th century but part of it became a Russian protectorate after the Russo-Turkish war of 1829. In 1861-62 the principalities of *Moldavia* and *Wallachia* were united and given the new name of Rumania. Rumania gained full independence in 1881 as a kingdom. During World War II German troops occupied the country but surrendered to Russia in 1944. A communist regime was set up after the war and a people's republic proclaimed in 1947.

RUSSIA: former name of the *USSR*. The term Russia applies to the Russian Empire until 1917 and correctly now to the *Russian Soviet Fedederated Socialist Republic,* though still commonly used to denote USSR.

RUSSIAN SOVIET FEDERATED SOCIALIST REPUBLIC: see *Russian Soviet Federative Socialist Republic*.

RUSSIAN SOVIET FEDERATIVE SOCIALIST REPUBLIC: the most important in size and political power of the fifteen Soviet Socialist Republics. The area historically known as *Russia* was ruled by the Romanov dynasty from 1613 until 1917. The Russo-Turkish wars of the 18th and 19th centuries greatly expanded Russian territory at the expense of the Ottoman Empire. After Napoleon's repulsion from Moscow in 1812 Russia and Austria became the leading mid-European powers. Territorial expansion coupled with liberal reforms and the unpopular Russo-Japanese War (1904-5) let to the Revolution of 1905. Serious losses were suffered in World War I and after a spate of rebellions the Bolsheviks took power in November 1917. In the same year Russia was officially proclaimed the Russian Soviet Federated Socialist Republic. In 1922 it was united with the *Ukraine, Belorussia* and the Transcaucasian Republics to form the Union of Soviet Socialist Republics (*USSR*).

RWANDA: alternative name is *Ruanda*. The area was joined to *Burundi* in 1898 as a German colony. After World War I both countries were mandated to *Belgium* as Ruanda-Urundi. The mandate lasted until 1946, when the area fell under UN trusteeship. In 1961 a republic was proclaimed over Rwanda and on 1 July 1962 the area split into two independent countries, Rwanda and Burundi.

RYUKYU ISLANDS: composed of *Amami-Gunto, Okinawa* and *Sakishima*. They were part of the Japanese Empire from 1879. After World War II they were placed under a US military governor and only returned to *Japan* by the USA in May 1972.

S

SABA (Island): one of the *Leeward Islands*, part of the *Netherlands Antilles*.

SABAH: state belonging to the Federation of *Malaysia*, situated on the northern part of *Borneo* and formerly known as *North Borneo*.

SADO (Island): part of *Japan*.

SAFETY ISLANDS: also known by the French *Iles du Salut*. Off the coast of *French Guiana*, used as a penal settlement until 1938. Composed of Royale, Joseph and Devil's Islands, part of *French Guiana*.

SAINT CHRISTOPHER (Island): alternative name for part of *Saint Kitts-Nevis*.

SAINT CROIX (Island): part of the *Virgin Islands, (USA)*.

SAINT DOMINGUE (Island): former name of *Haiti*.

SAINT EUSTATIUS (Island): one of the *Leeward Islands*, part of *Netherlands Antilles*.

SAINT HELENA (Island): the British dependency of Saint Helena includes the islands of *Ascension* and *Tristan da Cunha*. Saint Helena was annexed by the Dutch in 1633 and in 1659 it was occupied by the British East India Company. In 1834 it became a British crown colony. Ascension was discovered by the Portuguese in 1501, taken by the British in 1815 and made a dependency of Saint Helena in 1922. The Tristan da Cunha group of islands was discovered by the Portuguese in 1506, annexed by Britain in 1816 and became a dependency of Saint Helena in 1938.

SAINT JOHN (Island): part of the *Virgin Islands, (USA)*.

SAINT JOSEPH (Island): part of *Canada*, (Ontario).

SAINT KITTS-NEVIS (Islands): alternative name of Saint Kitts is *Saint Christopher*. Islands within the *Leeward Islands*; also included is the small island of Sombrero. The British first arrived on Saint Kitts in 1623, and on *Nevis* in 1628. They became part of the colony of the Leeward Islands from 1871 to 1956. On 27 February 1967 together with *Anguilla* they became a self-governing state in association with Britain. Anguilla and Sombrero formally separated from St Kitts-Nevis-Anguilla associated State on 19 December 1980 and became a separate dependent territory of the *UK*.

SAINT LAWRENCE (Island): part of *USA*, (Alaska).

SAINT LUCIA (Island): one of the *Windward Islands*. After one futile attempt on the part of the British to settle the island it was the French who succeeded in 1660. The island was contested by British and French, and finally the British regained it in 1803. It formed part of the British Windward Islands colony from 1958 to 1959, and Saint Lucia achieved independence on 22 February 1979.

SAINT MARTIN (Island): alternative name is *Sint-Maarten*, the southern section of the island is part of the *Netherlands Antilles*, and the northern section is part of *Guadeloupe*.

SAINT-PIERRE AND MIQUELON (Islands): these islands were colonized by France in 1604. The British took them for short periods but they were finally returned to France in 1814. Local autonomy was granted in 1935.

SAINT THOMAS (Island): part of the *Virgin Islands, (USA)*.

SAINT VINCENT AND THE GRENADINES (Islands): includes the territory of the State of St Vincent and certain of the Grenadines, ie Bequia, Canouan, Mayreau, Mustique, Union Island, Petit St Vincent and Prune Island. St Vincent was discovered by Columbus in 1498. French and English occupied it alternately until 1783 when it was finally restored to Britain. On 1 June 1969 St Vincent became a self governing state in association with Britain and together with the Grenadines full independence was achieved on 27 October 1979.

SAIPAN (Island): one of the *Marianas Islands*, part of *Pacific Islands (USA)*.

SAKHALIN (Island): former name is *Karafuto*, part of *USSR* (North of Japan).

SAKISHIMA (Islands): a group in the *Ryukyu Islands*, part of *Japan*.

SAL (Island): part of *Cape Verde Islands*.

SALA Y GOMEZ (Island): rocky island in the south Pacific Ocean, east northeast of *Easter* Island, part of *Chile*.

SALSETTE (Island): part of *India*.

SALTANAT OMAN: see *Oman*.

SALVADOR: alternative name of *El Salvador*.

SAMAR (Island): one of the *Visayan Islands*, part of the *Philippines*.

SAMOA I SISIFO: see *Western Samoa*.

SAMOA ISLANDS: the eastern section is known as *American Samoa* and remains under US control; and the remaining section is independent *Western Samoa*, independent on 1 January 1962.

SAMOS (Island): part of *Greece*, in the Aegean Sea, sometimes included in the *Sporadhes* Islands.

SAMOTHRACE (Island): alternative name is *Samothraki*, part of *Greece*.

SAN AMBROSIO (Island): in the Pacific Ocean off the central coast of Chile near *San Felix*, part of *Chile*.

SAN CRISTOBAL (Island): alternative name is *Makira*, part of the *Solomon Islands*.

SAND (Island): part of *Midway Islands*.

SANDALWOOD (Island): former name of *Sumba*, one of the *Lesser Sunda Islands*, part of *Indonesia*.

SAN FELIX (Island): island near *San Ambrosio* in the Pacific Ocean off the central coast of Chile. Part of *Chile*.

SANGI ISLANDS: alternatively Sangihe Islands, in Indonesia northeast of the *Celebes* Island. Main islands are Sangihe, Siau, Tahulandang, and Biaro, part of *Indonesia*.

SAN JUAN ISLANDS: composed of San Juan, Orcas and Lopez, part of *USA*.

SAN MARINO: the world's smallest republic; in 1631 its independence was recognized by the Papacy. *Italy* and San Marino have had agreements of friendship and economic cooperation since 1862. Full name is *Repubblica di San Marino*.

SAN SALVADOR (Island): former name is *Watling*, part of the *Bahamas*.

SAN SALVADOR (Island): alternative names are *James* and *Santiago*, one of the *Galapagos Islands*, part of *Ecuador*.

SANTA CATALINA (Island): part of *USA*, (California).

SANTA CRUZ ISLANDS: in the western Pacific Ocean, north of *Vanuatu*. Main island is Ndeni administered by the *Solomon Islands*. Other islands are Vanikoro and Utupua plus smaller ones. Discovered in 1595 by Mendaña.

SANTA CRUZ (Island): alternative names are *Indefatigable* and *Chaves*, one of the *Galapagos Islands*, part of *Ecuador*.

SANTA INES (Island): in *Tierra del Fuego*, part of *Chile*.

SANTA ISABEL (Island): alternative name is *Ysabel*, part of *Solomon Islands*.

SANTA MAURA (Island): former name of *Leucas*, alternative name is *Levkas*; one of the *Ionian Islands*, part of *Greece*.

SANTIAGO (Island): alternative name for *São Tiago*, part of the *Cape Verde Islands*.

SANTIAGO (Island): alternative name for *San Salvador*, one of the *Galapagos Islands*, part of *Ecuador*.

SANTO (Island): alternative name for *Espiritu Santo*, part of *New Hebrides*.

SANTO ANTAO (Island): part of the *Cape Verde Islands*.

SANTO DOMINGO (Island): former name of *Dominican Republic* and also of the island of *Hispaniola*.

SAO JORGE (Island): one of the *Azores Islands*, part of *Portugal*.

SAO LUIS (Island): former name is *Maranhao*, part of *Brazil*.

SAO MIGUEL (Island): one of the *Azores Islands*, part of *Portugal*.

SAO NICOLAU (Island): one of the *Cape Verde Islands*.

SAO TIAGO (Island): alternative name is *Santiago*, one of the *Cape Verde Islands*.

SAO TOME AND PRINCIPE: composed of the islands off West Africa: Sao Tomé, *Principe*, Pedras Tinhosas and Rolas. The islands were discovered by the Portuguese in 1471. They were proclaimed a colony of Portugal in 1522, but the Dutch held the islands from 1641 to 1740, after which they were regained by Portugal. Independence was declared on 12 July 1975.

SAO VICENTE (Island): part of the *Cape Verde Islands*.

SARAWAK: the western strip of the island of *Borneo*, previously a British colony until it became part of *Malaysia* on 16 September 1963.

SARDEGNA (Island): alternative name of *Sardinia*, part of *Italy*.

SARDINIA (Island): alternative name is Sardegna. After 1720 under the House of Savoy a Kingdom was formed with Savoy, Piedmont and Nice. Its King, Victor Emmanuel II was proclaimed King of Italy in 1861. The island received administrative autonomy under the Republican constitution of Italy in 1947. Part of *Italy*. Also includes *Asinara*, Caprera, San Pietro and *La Maddalena* islands.

SAREMA (Island): former name is *Osel*, part of *USSR*.

SARK (Island): one of the *Channel Islands* administered by *Guernsey*.

SASKATCHEWAN: one of the twelve constituent provinces of *Canada*; the great wheat-farming area. In 1870 the Hudson's Bay Company ceded the area to the Canadian federation. It became part of the *Northwest Territories*, then a separate province in 1905.

SAUDI ARABIA: former name is *Arabia*, full name is *Al-Mamlaka al-'Arabiya as-Sa'udiya*. The Kingdom of Saudi Arabia was proclaimed on 20 September 1932, after the unification of its *Nejd* and *Hijaz* regions.

SAVAGE (Island): former name of *Niue*, dependency of *New Zealand*.

SAVAII (Island): part of *Western Samoa*.

SCORPANTO (Island): former name for *Karpathos*, one of the *Dodecanese Islands*, part of *Greece*.

SCHLESWIG-HOLSTEIN: these two former duchies occupied the southern part of the Jutland Peninsula. They became a subject of conflict between the Danes and the Germans and were ceded to the German states as a result of a war in 1864. By the Treaty of Prague in 1866 Schleswig-Holstein was placed under Prussian rule. In 1921 part of the northern region was returned to *Denmark* after a plebiscite.

SCHWEIZ: alternative (German) name for *Switzerland*.

SCILLY ISLES: off Lands End, southwest *England*, group of many small islands, part of *UK*.

SCOTLAND: Originally the area was called Caledonia by the Romans but in the 4th and 5th century the Irish Celts, called Scots, settled and renamed the area Scotland. After frequent border wars relative peace was achieved in 1603 when King James VI of Scotland became James I of England thus uniting the two Kingdoms. The formal union of *England* and Scotland occurred in 1707 when the official name of the Island became Great Britain.

SELANGOR: one of the eleven federated states of West *Malaysia* on the Malay peninsula; it was created in 1742 by the Bugis princes who came from the *Celebes*. The British took the side of the Malays in the Malay-Bugis wars and after the founding of the Straits Settlements in 1826 Selangor accepted a British Adviser. In 1896 it joined *Pahang, Perak* and *Negri Sembilan* to form the Federated States of Malaya. It became a member state of the Malayan Union after World War II, the Federation of *Malaya* in 1948 and eventually the Federation of Malaysia in 1963. Selangor is the seat of the Federal Capital of Kuala Lumpur.

SENEGAL: in the 17th century the Portuguese were displaced by the Dutch and the French. The French influence extended to a large part of the area. In the 18th century Britain captured many of the French posts, but France held the administration and in 1895 it became part of *French West Africa* as a French colony. In 1958 the area became autonomous within the French Community and joined the Mali Federation in 1959. The federation broke up on 20 August 1960, and Senegal continued as an independent state. The 1963 constitution makes Senegal a presidential republic. Full name is *République du Sénégal*.

SENJA (Island): part of *Norway*.

SERAM (Island): alternative name of *Ceram*, one of the *Moluccas Group*, part of *Indonesia*.

SERBIA: one of the six constituent republics of *Yugoslavia* since 1945. This region of the Balkan peninsula was annexed by the Turks in 1459 and remained under Turkish influence until in 1829 Russia made the Turks grant Serbia autonomy under Russian protection. Serbia's independence was recognized in 1878 by the Congress of Berlin and remained intact until the country was overrun in 1915. Serbia joined the Kingdom of the Serbs, Croats and Slovenes in 1918, which kingdom eventually became Yugoslavia.

SERENDIB (Island): former name of *Sri Lanka*.

SEVERNAYA ZEMLYA ISLANDS: composed of *Komsomolets, Oktyabrskoy Revolyutsii, Bolshevik* and Pioner, part of *USSR*.

SEYCHELLES: the islands were occupied by the French in the mid 18th century and captured by the British in 1794. They became a dependency of Mauritius in 1770, and were assigned to Great Britain in 1810. In 1903 they became a crown colony and gained their independence on 28 June 1976. Composed of *Mahé*, Praslin, Silhouette, La Digue, *Aldabra*, and many smaller islands.

SHABA: part of *Zaïre*, the area formerly known as *Katanga*.

SHAM: alternative name of *Syrian Arab Republic*.

SHARJAH: one of the federation of *United Arab Emirates* since 1971, it was formerly a British protectorate.

SHEEP ISLANDS: alternative name is *Faroe Isalnds*.

SHEPPEY (Island): island in the mouth of the Thames River in *England*. Part of Kent County, *UK*.

SHETLAND ISLANDS: alternative name is *Zetland*. Orkney and Shetland Islands were originally ruled by Norway, the islands were pledges to James III of Scotland as security for dowry of Margaret, James's Queen in 1468. The pledge was not redeemed and the islands were annexed to Scotland in 1472. Composed of *Mainland, Unst, Yell, Fetlar, Bressay, Whalsay*, East and West *Burra, Fair Isle* and *Papa Stour*. Part of the *UK*.

SHIKOKU (Island): part of *Japan*.

SHUMAGIN ISLANDS: composed of Unga, Popof and Nagai, part of *USA*.

SIAM: name used for *Thailand* before 1939 and between 1945 and 1949.

SIBERUT (Island): part of *Indonesia*.

SICILIA (Island): alternative name for *Sicily*, part of *Italy*.

SICILY (Island): alternative name is *Sicilia*, part of *Italy*.

SIERRA LEONE: in the early 17th century British traders were active along the coast. In 1792 a new colony named Freetown was controlled by the Sierra Leone Company. In 1808 the British government took over the area. On 27 April 1961 the area became independent and on 19 April 1971 the country was declared a republic.

SIKKIM: a constitutional monarchy which was made an associated state of *India* in 1974. The monarch or 'chogyal' has been replaced by an Indian-appointed president.

SIMEULUE (Island): part of *Indonesia*.

SINAI PENINSULA: the peninsula north-east of Egypt which was included in *Israel* from 10 June 1967 to 25 April 1982 when Israel completed the withdrawal to the 1967 frontiers.

SINGAPORE: alternative name is *Singapura*. The island was secured by Sir Stamford Raffles in 1819. In 1824 Singapore came under British rule and, apart from a short period during World War II, remained so. In 1946 it was constituted with *Christmas Island* and the *Cocos (Keeling) Islands* as a crown colony. Singapore separated from them in June 1959 to become a self-governing state. In August 1963 it merged with *Malaysia* but separated on 9 August 1965 and became an independent republic. Full name is *Republic of Singapore*.

SINGAPURA: alternative name for *Singapore*.

SINT-MAARTEN (Island): alternative name for *Saint Martin*. The southern section of the island is part of the *Netherlands Antilles* and the northern section is part of *Guadeloupe*.

SJAELLAND (Island): alternative name for *Zealand*, part of *Denmark*.

SKOMER (Island): island in the Atlantic Ocean off the west coast of Pembroke, *Wales*, part of the *UK*.

SKYE (Island): one of the *Inner Hebrides*, off the coast of *Scotland*, part of *UK*.

SLOVENIA: one of the six constituent republics of *Yugoslavia* since 1945. Until 1918 the region was mainly contained in the Austrian crown lands of Carinthia, Carniola and Styria. From 1335 to 1918 Slovenia was part of *Austria*. In 1918 it joined the Kingdom of the Serbs, Croats and Slovenes (called Yugoslavia after 1929).

SNAKE (Island): former name of *Anguilla*.

SOCIALIST FEDERAL REPUBLIC OF YUGOSLAVIA: see *Yugoslavia*.

SOCIALIST PEOPLE'S LIBYAN ARAB REPUBLIC: see *Libya*.

SOCIALIST REPUBLIC OF VIETNAM: see *Vietnam*.

SOCIETY ISLANDS: composed of *Tahiti, Moorea, Raiatea* and many smaller islands, part of *French Polynesia*.

SOCIJALISTICKA FEDERATIVNA REPUBLIKA JUGOSLAVIJE: see *Yugoslavia*.

SOCORRO (Island): one of the *Revilla Gigedo Islands* in the Pacific Ocean off the coast of Colima, part of *Mexico*.

SOCOTRA (Island): alternative name is *Suqutra*, part of *Yemen*. It was a British Protectorate from 1886 to 1967 when it became part of Yemen.

SOLOMON ISLANDS: former name is *British Solomon Islands*. In 1885 German New Guinea established control over the northern section of the Solomon Islands, and the southern section became a British Protectorate in 1893. Australia occupied *Bougainville* and *Buka* during World War I. Bougainville and Buka now belong to *Papua New Guinea*. The islands became independent on 7 July 1978. They are composed of: *Choiseul, Guadalcanal, Malaita, San Cristobal, Santa Isabel, New Georgia, Ontong Java Islands*, and *Santa Crux Islands* and are administered by the Solomon Islands.

SOMALIA: former names are *British Somaliland* and *Italian Somaliland*, full names are *Somali Democratic Republic* and *Al-Jamhuuriyadda Dimuqraadiga Soomaliya*. France first acquired a foothold in the area in the 1860s, and Britain penetrated the area in 1884. Italy asserted its authority in 1889. During World War II the British took over the Italian section and held the combined regions until 1950. The area achieved internal autonomy as Somalia in 1956 and became independent on 1 July 1960. The French section became *Afars and Issas* then *Djibouti*.

SOMALI DEMOCRATIC REPUBLIC: see *Somalia*.

SOMERSET (Island): part of *Canada*, (Northwest Territory).

SOMERS ISLANDS: former name of *Bermuda*.

SOUTH AFRICA: alternative name is *Suid-Afrika*, full names are *Republic of South Africa* and *Republick van Suid-Afrika*. Former name is the *Union of South Africa*, which was the name of the area between 1910 to 1961. Names before the formation of the Union are: *Cape of*

Good Hope (colony) from 1795 to 1910; *Natal Republic* from 1843 to 1910; *Transvaal Republic*, also known as *South African Republic*, from 1853 to 1877 and 1880 to 1902 (this latter area then became a crown colony until 1910); *Orange River Sovereignty* from 1848 to 1854 under the British, *Orange Free State Republic* from 1854 to 1902 under the Boers and *Orange River Colony* from 1902 to 1910 under the British. These four states (Cape of Good Hope, Natal, Orange Free State, Transvaal) joined to form the Union of South Africa as an independent British Dominion, becoming the Republic of South Africa on 31 May 1961. *South West Africa* was mandated to South Africa in 1919. *Transkei* became an independent homeland on 26 October 1976; *Bophuthatswana* on 6 December 1977 and *Venda* on 13 September 1979. *Walvis Bay* is an enclave which forms part of South Africa.

SOUTH AFRICAN REPUBLIC: alternative name is *Transvaal Republic*, former name of part of *South Africa*.

SOUTHAMPTON (Island): part of *Canada*, (Northwest Territory).

SOUTH ANDAMAN (Island): one of the *Andaman* islands, part of *India*.

SOUTH ARABIA: former name of *South Yemen*, the name South Arabia was used from 1963 to 1967, followed by Southern Yemen from 1967 to 1970 and South Yemen from 1970. It is now the *People's Democratic Republic of Yemen*.

SOUTH AUSTRALIA: one of the constituent states and territories of *Australia*, South Australia became a British province in 1836. In 1901 it became a federated state of Australia.

SOUTH CAROLINA: first colonized in the 16th century, the Carolinas were split into North and South in 1713. In 1729 South Carolina became one of the Thirteen Colonies held by the British crown. It won independence in the American revolution and in 1788 was the 8th state to ratify the Constitution of the new confederation of the *USA*.

SOUTH DAKOTA: part of the Dakotas region was acquired by the *USA* in the Louisiana Purchase of 1803, the southeastern half being ceded to the USA by Britain in 1818. In 1861 Dakota Territory was set up, embracing the Dakotas North and South and neighbouring lands. In 1889 they were split into separate states and South Dakota became the 40th member state of the USA.

SOUTHERN AFRICA: undefined region, it is generally taken to include *Angola, Zambia, Zimbabwe, Mozambique, Botswana, Namibia, Malawi, Lesotho, South Africa*, and *Swaziland*.

SOUTHERN RHODESIA: former name of *Zimbabwe*.

SOUTH GEORGIA (Island): part of the *Falkland Island Dependencies*.

SOUTH ISLAND: part of *New Zealand*.

SOUTH KOREA: alternative names are *Republic of Korea* or *Han Kook*. Part of *Korea* until its partition after World War II into Russian (North) and American (South) occupied zones. Under UN observation elections led to the establishment of the Republic of Korea on 15 August 1948, when US military rule ended. *Cheju* island belongs to South Korea.

SOUTH ORKNEY (Islands): part of *British Antarctic Territory*.

SOUTH SANDWICH (Islands): part of the *Falkland Island Dependencies*.

SOUTH SHETLAND (Islands): part of *British Antarctic Territory*.

SOUTH UIST (Island): one of the *Outer Hebrides*, off the northwest coast of *Scotland*, part of the *UK*.

SOUTH VIETNAM: former name of southern *Vietnam*. Name used between 1954 and 1976; the name Vietnam was in use between 1945 and 1954 and after 1976.

SOUTH WEST AFRICA: alternative name for *Namibia*.

SOUTH YEMEN: former name of *People's Democratic Republic of Yemen*. Name still in use, see *Yemen*.

SOVIET UNION: alternative name for *USSR*.

SOYUZ SOVYETSKIKH SOTSIALISTICHESKIKH RESPUBLIK: see *Union of Soviet Socialist Republics*.

SPAIN: full name is *Estado Español*. The 16th century was the height of Spain's world power and of the Inquisition, and it was at this time that many colonies were acquired. After the war of Spanish Succession from 1701 to 1714 more and more colonies were lost to the Netherlands, Britain and France until in 1808 Bonaparte was put on the Spanish throne. In 1814 the British expelled the French from Spain and the monarchy was restored. Other Spanish possessions in South America gained independence and the remainder of the Empire was lost after the Spanish American war of 1898. In 1931 the monarchy was abolished and a dictatorship was set up under Franco after 1939. In 1975 when Franco died a constitutional monarchy was restored. Spanish enclaves in Africa are *Melilla* and *Ceuta* in *Morocco* and *Spanish North Africa*. The *Balearic Islands, Chaf Arinas*, and the *Canary Islands* are controlled by Spain.

SPANISH GUINEA: former name of *Equatorial Guinea*.

SPANISH MOROCCO: former name of a section of *Morocco*.

SPANISH NORTH AFRICA: an enclave of *Spain*, consisting of settlements on the Moroccan seaboard: Altracemas, Penon de la Gomera and the Chafarinas islands.

SPANISH SAHARA: former name of *Western Sahara*.

SPICE ISLANDS: alternative name for the *Moluccas Group*, part of *Indonesia*.

SPITSBERGEN (Island): former name is *Vestspitsbergen*, largest island in the *Svalbard* group, part of *Norway*.

SPORADES (Islands): two groups of islands in the Aegean Sea, Northern Sporades and Southern Sporades. The name applies in its broadest sense to all Greek Islands of the Aegean outside of the Cyclades. In antiquity the name applied to the scattered isles of the southeast Aegean generally including the *Dodecanese* Islands, Icaria and *Samos* and sometimes *Chios* and *Lesbos*. The Northern Sporades are a little more definite and include Skyros, Skopelos, Skiathos and Iliodhrómia, plus smaller islands. Part of *Greece*.

SRI LANKA: former names are *Serendib* and *Ceylon*. The Portuguese conquered the coast in the 16th century and by the mid-17th century the Dutch had taken over. In 1795 the Dutch possessions were occupied by the British, who made the island the crown colony of Ceylon in 1798. Full independence was granted to the island as a dominion on 4 February 1948. The island was declared the Republic of Sri Lanka in 1972 and on 3 March 1978 the long form of the name became the Democratic Socialist Republic of Sri Lanka.

STATEN (Island): part of *USA*, (New York).

STATE OF ISRAEL: see *Israel*.

STATE OF QATAR: see *Qatar*.

STATO DELLA CITTA DEL VATICANO: see *Vatican City*.

STEFANSSON (Island): part of *Canada*, (Northwest Territory).

STEWART (Island): part of *New Zealand*.

STADBROKE (Island): island off the southeast coast of Queensland, *Australia*, of which it is part.

STREYMOY (Island): alternative name is *Strømø*, largest of the Faroe Islands.

STROMO (Island): alternative name of *Streymoy* Island, largest of the *Faroe Islands*.

SUDAN: former name is *Anglo-Egyptian Sudan*. North-east Sudan, called Nubia in ancient times, was conquered by the Egyptians in the 19th century who made Khartoum their headquarters. The British supported Egypt in trying to extend their influence further south in 1881. The local Mahdists prevailed and Britain and Egypt withdrew. In the 1890s Britain again intervened to destroy the power of the Madhists and formed the condominium government of Anglo-Egyptian Sudan in 1899. Sudan achieved independence on 1 January 1956, declaring itself the *Democratic Republic of the Sudan*. Alternative full name is *Jumhouriya al-Sudan al-Democratiya*.

SUDEST (Island): alternative name for *Tagula*, in the *Louisiade Archipelago*, part of *Papua New Guinea*.

SUID-AFRIKA: alternative name for *South Africa*.

SUISSE: alternative (French) name for *Switzerland*.

SULA (Islands): composed of *Taliabu*, Sanana and Mangole, in the *Moluccas Group*, part of *Indonesia*.

SULAWESI (Island): alternative name of *Celebes*, one of the *Greater Sunda Islands*, part of *Indonesia*.

SULU ARCHIPELAGO: composed of Jolo, Pangutaran, Samales, Tawitawi, Tapul and Sibutu, part of the *Philippines*.

SUMATRA (Island): one of the *Greater Sunda Islands*, part of *Indonesia*.

SUMBA (Island): former name is *Sandalwood*, one of the *Lesser Sunda Islands*, part of *Indonesia*.

SUMBAWA (Island): one of the *Lesser Sunda Islands*, part of *Indonesia*.

SUOMEN TASAVALTA: see *Finland*.

SUOMI-FINLAND: alternative name of *Finland*.

SUQUTRA: alternative name of *Socotra*, part of *Yemen*.

SURINAM: or Suriname; former names are *Dutch Guiana* or *Netherlands Guiana*. Dutch expeditions to the area first started in 1597 and present day *Guyana* was settled in 1616. Dutch control was interrupted by British and French attacks in the 18th century. In 1815 the area of Guyana was given to the British, and Surinam to the Dutch as Dutch Guiana. Full independence was achieved on 25 November 1975.

SVALBARD (Islands): largest island is *Spitsbergen*. Norway took sovereignty of these islands in the Arctic Ocean in 1925. Composed of *West Spitsbergen, North-East Land*, East Island, Barents Island, Prince Charles Foreland and smaller islands.

SVERIGE: alternative name for *Sweden*.

SVIZZERA: alternative (Italian) name for *Switzerland*.

SWAZILAND: the British arrived in the area in 1888 and in 1903 the area became a High Commission Territory. On 6 September 1968 the Kingdom of Swaziland achieved complete independence.

SWEDEN: alternative name is *Sverige;* full name is *Konungariket Sverige*. In the 17th century Sweden was a dominant Protestant power in Europe. Wars with Russia and Poland led to added land for Sweden. Wars in the 19th century resulted in loss of land but in gaining *Norway* which was a separate kingdom in union with Sweden until 1905. It has been a monarchy since the 12th century. *Gotland* and *Oland* are part of Sweden.

SWITZERLAND: also known as the Swiss Confederation; alternative names are *Schweiz, Suisse* and *Svizzera*. In 1515 neutrality became the basis of Swiss policy and European powers recognized their independence in the mid-17th century. The republic of Switzerland maintained armed neutrality throughout both World Wars.

SYDNEY (Island): former name of *Manra* Island, one of the *Phoenix Islands*, part if *Kiribati*.

SYRIA: full names are Syrian Arab Republic and *Al-Jumhouriya al-Arabiya as-Souriya*. In 1832 Syria was annexed to *Egypt* until 1840 when it was forced to return to the Ottomans. Britain and France occupied Syria in 1941 and an independent republic was proclaimed on 1 January 1944. In February 1958 Syria joined the *United Arab Republic* and left again in 1961, to remain the Syrian Arab Republic.

T

TABUAERAN (Island): former name is *Fanning* Island, one of the *Line Isalnds*, part of *Kiribati*.

TADZHIK SOVIET SOCIALIST REPUBLIC: or Tadzhikistan. One of the fifteen constituent republics of the *USSR*. This central Asian region came under Russian control in the late 19th century. The Red Army did not establish full control over the Tadzhik rebels until 1921. It became an autonomous republic with *Uzbekistan* in 1924 and a constituent republic of the USSR in 1929.

TAGULA (Island): alternative name is *Sudest*, in the *Louisiade Archipelago*, part of *Papua New Guinea*.

TAHITI (Island): one of the *Society Islands*, part of *French Polynesia*.

TAIWAN: former name is *Formosa*, full name is *Republic of China*, former unofficial name is *Nationalist China*. The Portuguese reached the island in 1590 and named it Formosa. In 1624 the Dutch and Spanish established bases on the island but by 1641 the Dutch controlled the entire island. China seized the island in 1662 and established a kingdom; another change occurred in 1683 when the Manchus took control. Japan took the island in 1895 and it was returned to China in 1945. In 1949 when Communist China took control of the mainland the nationalist government took refuge on Taiwan. In 1979 it restored diplomatic relations with Peking.

TALAUD (Islands): also called Talaur Islands in the Pacific Ocean northeast of the Celebes Isalnds, part of *Indonesia*. Composed of Karakelong, Salebabu, Kaburuang and other smaller islands.

TALIABU (Island): one of the *Sula* Islands in the *Moluccas Group*, part of *Indonesia*.

TAMIL NADU: one of the twenty-one states of *India*, the region that is now Tamil Nadu was conquered by the British in the mid-18th century and formed part of the presidency of Madras. It became a separate state in 1947 but lost territory to *Andhra Pradesh* in 1953 and *Karnataka* in 1956.

TANGANYIKA: former name of part of *Tanzania*.

TANIMBAR (Islands): composed of *Yamdena*, Selami and Larat in the *Moluccas Group*, part of *Indonesia*.

TANZANIA: or *United Republic of Tanzania*; former names are *German East Africa* and *Tanganyika*. In 1506 the Portuguese controlled most of the coastal area but were expelled by local inhabitants. By the early 19th century, Arab traders had settled the area. Germany established a sphere of influence in 1886 and formed the German East

Africa Company. Other neighbouring countries were added to German East AFrica. After World War I Tanganyika was placed under British mandate until its independence on 9 December 1961. It became the Republic of Tanganyika in December 1962 and on 23 April 1964 *Zanzibar* and Tanganyika merged to form one united republic called Tanzania. *Pemba* Island is part of Tanzania.

TARAWA (Island): part of *Kiribati*.

TASMANIA: an island state, one of the constituent states and territories of Australia. It was colonized by the British in 1825 and in 1901 joined the Australian Commonwealth. Former name is *Van Diemen's Land*. Tasmania administers *Macquarie* Island.

TCHAD: alternative name for *Chad*.

TENERIFE (Island): or Teneriffe, part of *Spain*.

TENNESSEE: early French settlers encountered several Indian tribes in the Tennessee region and French claims were lost to English colonizers after the French and Indian wars (1763). After the American Revolution the area became the Territory of the United States South of the River Ohio, and in 1796 Tennessee emerged as the 16th member state of the confederation of the *USA*.

TERAINA (Island): former name is *Washington* Island, one of the *Line Islands*, part of *Kiribati*.

TERCEIRA (Island): one of the *Azores Islands*, part of *Portugal*.

TERENGGANU: one of the eleven federated states of *West Malaysia* on the Malay peninsula, it was one of the four northern kingdoms which fell under Siamese influence from the 16th century. Under the Anglo-Siamese treaty of 1826 it remained under Siamese control, but was regained by Britain in 1909. With the other northern states of *Kedah, Kelantan* and *Perlis*, (and *Johore*) it became part of the Unfederated Malay States. After World War II Terengganu joined the Malayan Union, then the Federation of *Malaya* in 1948 and the Federation of Malaysia in 1963.

TERNATE (Island): in the *Moluccas Group*, part of *Indonesia*.

TERRES AUSTRALES ET ANTARCTIQUES FRANCAISES: part of *Antarctica*.

TEXAS: the second largest state (to *Alaska*) of the *USA*, it was the 28th to join the confederation, in 1845. Texas was settled in the 17th century by the Spanish and two centuries later Americans moved in from the north, soon outnumbering Mexican settlers from the south. Texas declared its independence in 1836 and remained an independent republic until admission to the confederated USA.

THAILAND: full name is *Prathet Thai, Muang-Thai* or *Prades Thai*; former name was *Siam*. In the 19th century France had an empire in *Indochina* excluding Siam, whilst Britain held *Malaya* and *Burma*. In this way Siam was a buffer state between the two countries. The name changed to Thailand in 1939 but it reverted to Siam in 1945. Another change of government led to the name Thailand being used after 1949. Thailand is a constitutional monarchy.

THASOS (Islands): part of *Greece*.

TIBET: an autonomous region of China since 1951, it was virtually an independent country from 1911 to 1950. *Sikkim* was detached from Tibet in 1890 by Britain.

TIBURON (Island): part of *Mexico*.

TIDORE (Island): in the *Moluccas Group*, part of *Indonesia*.

TIERRA DEL FUEGO (Islands): formerly King Charlie South Land. Composed of *Navarino, Hoste, Clarence, Santa Inés* and Desolation, the eastern section is part of *Argentina* and the western section part of *Chile*.

TIMOR (Island): new name of *East Timor* and *West Timor* together. One of the *Lesser Sunda Islands*, part of *Indonesia*.

TINIAN (Island): one of the *Marianas Islands*, part of the *Pacific Islands (USA)*.

TOBAGO (Island): part of *Trinidad and Tobago*.

TOGO: former name is *French Togoland*. Germany settled the area in the 19th century but after World War I the area was divided into *British Togoland* and *French Togoland*. British Togoland joined the *Gold Coast* to become independent *Ghana* on 6 March 1957. French Togoland was joined with *Dahomey* (*Benin*) from 1934 to 1937, then separated and became the Republic of Togo in 1957, gaining independence on 27 April 1960. Full name is *République Togolaise*.

TOKELAU (Islands): composed of Atafu, Nukunono and Fakaofo. Alternative name is *Union Isles*. Discovered in 1765 by the British. In 1927 they were placed under the administration of *Western Samoa* as part of the *New Zealand* mandate.

TONGA: former name is *Friendly Islands*. They were discovered in 1616 by the British. A constitutional monarchy was established by the British in 1862 and has been self-governing under British protection since 1900. Independence was gained on 4 June 1970. Area composed of three main groups: *Tongatapu*, Vavau and Haapai.

TONGATAPU (Island): part of the *Tonga Islands*.

TONKIN: former name of the central part of *Vietnam*. Still in use as Gulf of Tonkin.

TORTOLA (Island): part of the *British Virgin Islands*.

TRAILL (Island): part of *Greenland*.

TRANGAN (Island): one of the *Aru* Islands in the *Moluccas Group*, part of *Indonesia*.

TRANS-JORDAN: former name of *Jordan*.

TRANSKEI: an independent homeland created on 26 October 1976 in the *Republic of South Africa*.

TRANSVAAL REPUBLIC: alternative name is *South African Republic*, former name of part of *South Africa*.

TRES MARIAS ISLANDS: in the Pacific Ocean off the coast of Nayarit, *Mexico*. Composed of Maria Cleófas, Maria Magdalena, and Maria Madre, part of *Mexico*.

TRINIDAD AND TOBAGO: Trinidad was discovered by Columbus in 1498. The two islands received a formal title in 1802 and were settled in the next year. They were joined politically in 1888 and only became independent on 31 August 1962.

TRIPURA: one of the twenty-one states of *India*, the Tripura area was won by the British from the Moguls in the 19th century and incorporated into the *Union of India* in 1949 as part of *Assam*. It became a union territory in 1956 and a state in 1972.

TRISTAN DA CUNHA (Islands): Tristan da Cunha is the only inhabitable island in a group of volcanic islands. The group is a dependency of *Saint* Helena. Other islands in the group are Inaccessible Island, the Nightingale Islands and Gough Island.

TROBRIAND ISLANDS: composed of Kiriwana Island and many smaller ones, part of *Papua New Guinea*.

TRUCIAL OMAN: former name of the *United Arab Emirates*.

TRUCIAL STATES: former name of the *United Arab Emirates*.

TRUK (Islands): composed of Tol, Moen, Fefan, Dublon, Udot, Uman, Kuop and many smaller islands, in the *Caroline Islands*, part of *Pacific Islands (USA)*.

TUAMOTU ISLANDS: alternative name is Low Archipelago. Discovered in 1606 by the Spanish and annexed in 1881 by the French. Part of *French Polynesia*. Includes the islands in the *Actaeon Group*. Chief islands are Makatéa, Fakarava, Rangiroa, Anaa, Hao, and Reao plus many smaller islands.

TUBUAI ISLANDS: alternative name is Austral Islands. Discovered in 1777 by Captain Cook and annexed in 1880 by France. Composed of Rimatara, Rurutu, Tubuai, Raevavae, Rapa plus smaller islands. Part of *French Polynesia*.

TUNISIA: full name is *Al-jumhouriya Attunisia*. In the 14th century Tunisia was controlled by the Turkish beys of the *Ottoman Empire* but attained virtual independence. The country's accumulation of heavy debts caused European intervention in the 19th century and the area became a French protectorate. In 1950 a certain autonomy was granted and full independence was achieved on 20 March 1956. The country became a republic in 1957. *Djerba* island is part of Tunisia.

TURKEY: full name is *Türkiye Cumhuriyeti*. The *Ottoman Empire* was founded in the 13th century and ruled vast areas until its dissolution in 1918. The Ottoman Turks expanded from a small Turkish State to include the Byzantine Empire and the *Balkan States*. Expansion reached a peak in the 16th century when many countries felt the influence of the Ottomans. At the turn of the 17th century the disintegration started and territory was lost. The Russo-Turkish wars of the 18th and 19th centuries led to the independence of many areas. In 1922 modern Turkey emerged and proclaimed itself a republic on 29 October 1923. *Gokceada* island is part of Turkey.

TURKISH CYPRIOT FEDERATED STATE: see *Cyprus*.

TURKIYE CUMHURIYETI: see *Turkey*.

TURKMEN SOVIET SOCIALIST REPUBLIC: or Turkmenistan. One of the fifteen constituent republics of the *USSR* since 1925, it was only formed in 1924.

TURKS AND CAICOS ISLANDS: the islands were discovered in 1512 but uninhabited until the British settled the area in 1766. They were annexed to Jamaica in 1873 and are now a dependency of Britain. Composed of *Grand Caicos,* Grand Turk and many smaller islands.

TUTUILA (Island): largest island of *American Samoa*.

TUVALU: former name is *Ellice Islands*, the name changed with independence on 1 October 1978. The islands were a British protectorate from 1892 to 1915 when they were included in the *Gilbert and Ellice Islands* colony. The Ellice Islands left the colony on 1 October 1975. Composed of *Funafuti* and many smaller islands.

U

UBANGI-SHARI: former name of the *Central African Empire*.

UGANDA: former name is *Buganda*. The area was first visited by Europeans in 1862. In 1890 British authority was established in southern Uganda and the area was officially made a protectorate in 1894. On 9 October 1962 the area became independent and in 1963 it was made a republic.

UK: see *United Kingdom of Great Britain and Northern Ireland*.

UKRAINIAN SOVIET SOCIALIST REPUBLIC: one of the fifteen constituent republics of the *USSR* and second largest in terms of population. The term 'Ukraine' came into general use in the 16th century. The Ukrainians fought for a long time against Polish and Russian domination and the country proclaimed independence in 1918 after the Russian revolution of 1917. In 1922 it joined the USSR. During and after World War II the territories of Bessarabia, eastern Galicia, northern Bukovina and Ruthenia (Transcarpathia) were added to Ukrainian territory. The Ukraine has its own seat at the UN.

ULSTER: an alternative name in common use for *Northern Ireland*, though it correctly describes the three counties of Cavan, Donegal and Monaghan (all in the *Irish Republic*) as well as the six counties which make up Northern Ireland.

UMM AL-QAIWAIN: one of the seven federated *United Arab Emirates* since 1971, it was formerly a British protectorate.

UMNAK (Island): one of the *Fox Islands*, in the *Aleutian Islands*, part of *USA*.

UNALASKA (Island): one of the *Fox Islands*, in the *Aleutian Islands*, part of *USA*.

UNGUJA (Island): alternative name for *Zanzibar*, part of *Tanzania*.

UNIMAK (Island): one of the *Fox Islands*, in the *Aleutian Islands*, part of *USA*.

UNION (Islands): alternative name for *Tokelau Islands*, administered by *Western Samoa* as part of the *New Zealand* mandate.

UNION OF INDIA: see *India*.

UNION OF SOUTH AFRICA: former name of the *Republic of South Africa*.

UNION OF SOVIET SOCIALIST REPUBLICS: full name is *Soyuz Sovyetskikh Sotsialisticheskikh Respublik*, former name is *Russia*, alternative name is *Soviet Union*. The Russian Empire expanded at the expense of the *Ottoman Empire* in the 18th century. Expansion continued in the 19th century. The revolution of 1917 overthrew the monarchy and the Soviet regime emerged as the *Russian Soviet Federated Socialist Republic.* In 1922 this was united with several neighbouring republics to form the USSR. The fifteen Union Republics that now comprise the USSR are: *RSFR* and *Ukrainian, Belorussian, Uzbek, Kazakh, Georgian Azerbaidjan, Lithuanian, Moldavian, Latvian, Kirghiz, Tadzhik, Armenian, Turkmen* and *Estonian Soviet Socialist Republics.* Islands that are part of USSR are: *Bolshoy Shantar, Bering, Karagin, Khiuma, Kolguyev, Sakhalin, Sarema, Vaygach, Wrangel, Zemlya Georga* and *Zemlya Aleksandry.* Island groups are: *Severnaya Zemlya Islands, Kuril Islands, Novaya Zemlya* and *New Siberian Islands.*

UNITED ARAB EMIRATES: former names are *Trucial Oman, Trucial States* and *Pirate Coast.* The Trucial States were bound by truce with Britain in 1820 and by an agreement in 1892 accepting protection. After a period of internal autonomy they became an independent federation of states on 2 December 1971, with *Ras al-Khaimah* the 7th emirate to join the federation on 10 February 1972. The other six emirates are: *Abu Dhabi, Ajman, Dubai, Fujairah, Sharjah* and *Umm al-Qaiwain.*

UNITED ARAB REPUBLIC: a political union was made between *Egypt* and *Syria* in 1958. On 5 October 1961 Syria withdrew and the union thus ended. *North Yemen* also joined the union from 1958 to 1961, to form a loose federation called the United Arab States.

UNITED KINGDOM OF GREAT BRITAIN AND NORTHERN IRE—LAND: the term *Great Britain* or *Britain* describes only *England, Scotland* and *Wales,* but is commonly used to refer to the UK as a whole. In 1535 King Henry VIII brought about the political union of England and Wales and in the Elizabethan age of the 16th century the great colonization of overseas areas began. In 1603 James I of England, who was also James VI of Scotland, united the two thrones, but the Act of Union only came about in 1707. In 1801 Great Britain and Ireland were united and the official title then became the Union of Great Britain and Ireland. A rebellion in Ireland (1916-21) led to the formation of the Irish Free State and *Northern Ireland* as separate entities. In 1927 the full name of the United Kingdom of Great Britain and Northern Ireland came into use. Islands under the UK are:
England: *Man, Wight, Scilly Isles, Channel Isles, Holy Isle, Lundy, Sheppy, Walney, Hayling.*
Northern Ireland: *Rathlin.*
Scotland: *Arran, Orkney Islands, Shetland Islands, The Hebrides, Bute, Cumbraes.*
Wales: *Holy, Anglesey, Bardsey, Caldy, Ramsey, Skomer.*
The dependent territories of UK are: *Anguilla, Bermuda, the British Antarctic Territory, British Indian Ocean Territory, British Virgin*

Islands, Brunei, Cayman Islands, Falkland Islands, Gibraltar, Hong Kong, Montserrat, Pitcairn Islands, St Helena (including Ascension and Tristan da Cunha), Turks and Caicos.

UNITED REPUBLIC OF TANZANIA: see Tanzania.

UNITED STATES OF AMERICA: in 1492 Columbus discovered America, the first of many explorers who came to the continent from France, Spain and England. The Spanish took control of the south, the French of the north and British colonies were founded in the central regions. The British had driven the French from the Great Lakes region by 1760. The American Revolution of 1775 to 1783 resulted in independence for the thirteen Brtish colonies. A central federal constitution was eventually promulgated in 1787. Over the following century the new federation expanded to include several more independent states. The American Civil War (1861-65) broke out when the Southern States wanted to secede and form themselves into a confederacy. The result was victory for the North and the end of all slavery. The USA entered World War II after the Pearl Harbour attack by the Japanese in 1941. The fifty member states of the USA are as follows: *Alabama, Alaska, Arizona, Arkansas, California, Colorado, Connecticut, Delaware, Florida, Georgia, Hawaii, Idaho, Illinois, Indiana, Iowa, Kansas, Kentucky, Louisiana, Maine, Maryland, Massachusetts, Michigan, Minnesota, Mississippi, Missouri, Montana, Nebraska, Nevada, New Hampshire, New Jersey, New Mexico, New York, North Carolina, North Dakota, Ohio, Oklahoma, Oregon, Pennsylvania, Rhode Island, South Carolina, South Dakota, Tennessee, Texas, Utah, Vermont, Virginia, Washington, West Virginia, Wisconsin, Wyoming*; and the *District of Columbia*. Islands belonging to the USA are: *Kodiak, Long, Manhattan, Marsh, Martha's Vineyard, Merritt, Mount Desert, Nantucket, Nelson, Nunivak, Padre, Royale, Saint Lawrence, Santa Catalina, Whidbey, Staten, Wake, Drummond, Afognak*. Island groups are: *San Juan Islands, Shumagin Islands, Aleutian Islands*, and *Alexander Archipelago*.

UNST (Island): one of the *Shetland Islands*, in *Scotland*, part of the *UK*.

UPOLU (Island): part of *Western Samoa*.

UPPER VOLTA: full name is *République de Haute-Volta*; alternative name is *Voltaic Republic*. France gained control over the area at the end of the 19th century. It was part of *French West Africa* and administered by Upper Senegal-Niger. It became a separate protectorate in 1919 but was administered as part of the *Ivory Coast* from 1932 to 1947. In 1947 Upper Volta was established as a territory within the French Union and achieved full independence on 5 August 1960. It became a Republic on 11 December 1958. A new constitution promulgated in 1970 was suspended in 1974. In 1984, its name was changed to *Bourkinn Fasso*.

URUGUAY: former name is *Banda Oriental*, full name is *Républica Oriental del Uruguay*. The first permanent settlement was established by the Spanish in 1624. The name Banda Oriental lasted into the 19th century when in 1825 a small group (the 'Thirty-three Immortals') declared it independent Uruguay. Britain helped the area to become an independent buffer state in the peace treaty of 1828. In 1830 a republic was inaugurated.

URUNDI: former name of *Burundi*.

USA: see *United States of America*.

USEDOM (Island): alternative name is *Uznam*, part of the *German Democratic Republic*.

USSR: see *Union of Soviet Socialist Republics*.

US TRUST TERRITORY OF THE PACIFIC: see *Pacific Islands (USA)*.

UTAH: first settled by the Spanish, it was a possession of Spain until acquired by the *USA* in 1848 after the Mexican War. In 1840 a large region embracing modern Utah was created Utah Territory. The creation of the territories of *Nevada*, *Colorado* and *Wyoming* reduced Utah to its present size and in 1896 it became the 45th state to join the confederation of the USA.

UTTAR PRADESH: one of the twenty-one states of *India*, Uttar Pradesh is the product of a merger in 1950 between the United Provinces and the princely states of Benares, Rampur and Tehri.

UZBEK SOVIET SOCIALIST REPUBLIC: or Uzbekistan. One of the fifteen constituent republics of the *USSR*. The Uzbek Empire broke up into separate principalities in the 17th century and was overrun by the Russians from 1865 to 1873. In 1924 the Uzbek SSR was formed and joined the USSR.

UZNAM (Island): alternative name for *Usedom*, part of the *German Democratic Republic*.

V

VALENTIA (Island): off the coast of County Kerry, *Irish Republic*. It is the eastern terminal of transatlantic cables, the first of which was laid in 1865. Part of the *Irish Republic*.

VALLS D'ANDORRA: see *Andorra*.

VANCOUVER (Island): part of *Canada*.

VAN DIEMEN'S LAND (Island): former name of *Tasmania*, part of *Australia*.

VANUA LEVU (Island): part of *Fiji*.

VANUATU (Islands): formerly *New Hebrides* or *Nouvelles Hébrides*. They were discovered by the Portuguese in 1606, and British missionaries arrived there in the early 19th century. In 1887 the islands were placed under an Anglo-French naval commission, and became a condominium in 1906. Independence as Vanuatu was achieved on 30 July 1980. The Vanuatu group comprises *Espiritu Santo, Efate, Malekula, Erromango* plus many smaller islands.

VATE (Island): alternative name for *Efate*, part of *Vanuatu*, formerly *New Hebrides*.

VATICAN CITY: full name is *Stato della Città del Vaticano*, alternative name is *Holy See*. The area is enclosed within the boundaries of Rome and has been an independent state with the Pope as absolute ruler since 11 February 1929.

VAYGACH (Island): part of *USSR* (southeast of Novaya Zemlya).

VEGLIA (Island): former name of *Krk*, part of *Yugoslavia*.

VENDA: an independent homeland created on 13 September 1979 in the *Republic of South Africa*.

VENDSYSSEL-THY (Island): usually regarded as part of the Danish mainland, but it is actually an island, since in 1825 the Lim Fjord of Kattegat Straight reached the North Sea cutting the peninsula in two. Part of *Denmark*.

VENEZUELA: in full *República de Venezuela*. Spanish settlements were established in the late 15th century. The area was included in the Spanish viceroyalty of *New Granada* from 1717 with modern *Panama, Colombia* and *Ecuador*. Venezuela became a captaincy-general of Spain, and was liberated by Bolivar in 1814. Complete independence from Spain was secured in 1821. *Margarita Island* comprises most of the state of Nueva Esparta with a few smaller islands within the Venezuelan Federation.

VERMONT: disputed between the British colonies of *New Hampshire* and *New York* in the 18th century, in 1777 Vermont proclaimed itself an independent state. It remained so for ten years and was not admitted to the new confederation of the *USA* until after its constitution had been adopted by the Thirteen Colonies; it was the 14th to join the Union, in 1791.

VESTERÅLEN ISLANDS: group in the Norwegian Sea off the northwest coast of Norway. Main islands are Hinnøy, Langøy and Andøya, part of *Norway*.

VESTSPITSBERGEN (Island): Norwegian name for *West Spitsbergen*, part of *Svalbard*.

VICTORIA: one of the constituent states and territories of the Commonwealth of *Australia* since it joined as a federated state in 1901. It had been made a British colony in 1851 and granted self-government in 1855.

VICTORIA (Island): part of *Canada*, (Northwest Territory).

VIEQUES (Island): alternative name is *Crab*, part of *Puerto Rico*.

VIETNAM: in 1859 the French captured Saigon and established the colony of *Cochin China*. In 1884 France declared protectorates over *Annam* and *Tonkin*. This area together with *Cambodia* formed *French Indochina*, to which *Laos* was added in 1893. After World War II independence within the French Union was granted and the name was changed to Vietnam until 1954. Communist influences built up in the north and the country split in two. *North Vietnam* was the *Democratic Republic of Vietnam* from 1954 to 1976 and *South Vietnam* was the Republic of Vietnam from 1954 to 1976. After the Vietnam war the country was reunified on 2 July 1976 and is now called the *Socialist Republic of Vietnam*. The alternative full name is *Công Hòa Xã Hôi Chu Nghia Viêt Nam*.

VIRGINIA: the name Virginia applied in the 16th century to the vast area of North America open to English colonization; not already in the hands of the French or Spanish. In 1624 the Jamestown region became the first of the thirteen English colonies in America, taking the name Virginia. It declared its independence in 1776 and was the first state to draft its own constitution. It joined the confederation of the *USA* in 1788 as its 10th member state.

VIRGIN ISLANDS (UK): alternative name is *British Virgin Islands*.

VIRGIN ISLANDS (USA): former name is *Danish West Indies*. The Virgin Islands as a whole were discovered by Columbus in 1493. The USA bought the Danish West Indies in 1917 and renamed them the Virgin Islands (USA). Composed of: *Saint Thomas, Saint Croix, Saint John* and many smaller islands.

VISAYAN ISLANDS: alternative name is *Bisayas*. Composed of *Bohol, Cebu, Leyte, Masbate, Negros, Panay, Samar* and many smaller islands, part of the *Philippines*.

VITI LEVU (Islands): part of *Fiji*.

VOLCANO ISLANDS: Japanese name is Kazan Retto or Iwo Retto. Group of three small islands south of Japan, comprise *Iwo Jima*, Kita Iwo and Minami Iwo. Administered by USA from 1945-1968, returned to *Japan* in 1968.

VOLTAIC REPUBLIC: alternative name of *Upper Volta*.

VORIAI SPORADHES ISLANDS: see *Sporadhes* (Islands).

VRANGELYA (Island): alternative name for *Wrangel*, part of the *USSR*.

W

WAIGEO (Island): one of the *Raja Ampat Islands* in the *West Irian Islands*, part of *Indonesia*.

WAKE (Island): discovered by the Spanish in 1568, Wake Island was annexed by the USA in 1898. It is a USA commercial air base.

WALES: the Anglo Saxon invasion of *England* did not at first affect Wales. They maintained their own culture until the 11th century when the Normans put pressure on the Welsh Princes. The conquest of Wales was completed in 1284 by Edward I. His son was proclaimed Prince of Wales in 1301, a title borne by the King's eldest son since then. Part of the *UK*.

WALLACHIA: see *Moldavia*.

WALLIS AND FUTUNA ISLANDS: former name of the *Futuna* Islands is *Hoorn Islands*. The islands came under French control in 1842 and achieved the status of a French Overseas Territory after a referendum on 27 December 1959.

WALNEY (Island): off the northwest coast of *England*, there is a connecting bridge with Barrow in Furness, Lancashire, part of the *UK*.

WALVIS BAY: in central *Namibia*, an enclave of the *Republic of South Africa*.

WASHINGTON: in the 18th century Washington and *Oregon* were together known as Columbia River country, and in 1818 the *USA* and Britain shared rights over the area. In 1853 the region was divided and Washington Territory came into being (including part of modern *Idaho*). In 1889 Washington became the 42nd state to be admitted to the Union.

WASHINGTON (Island): former name of *Teraina* Island, one of the *Line Islands*, part of *Kiribati*.

WATLING (Island): former name of *San Salvador*, part of *Bahamas*.

WELLINGTON (Island): off the coast of south *Chile* of which is it part.

WEST BANK: the area of Judea and Sumaria that was occupied by *Israel* on 10 June 1967.

WEST BENGAL: one of the twenty-one states of *India*, West Bengal came into being in 1947 when the former presidency of Bengal was partitioned between India and *Pakistan*. India retained the West Bengal section, including Calcutta.

WESTERN AUSTRALIA: first settled in 1829, Western Australia became one of the constituent federated states and territories of the Commonwealth of *Australia* in 1901.

WESTERN ISLANDS: alternative name for *Hebrides*, off the coast of *Scotland*, part of the *UK*.

WESTERN SAHARA: former name is *Spanish Sahara*, former names of parts of the area are Saguia el Hamra and Sekia el Hamra. Rio de Oro was part of Western Sahara. The Portuguese reached the area in 1434 and Spain claimed a protectorate over the coast in 1884. In April 1958 Spain joined Saguia el Hamra and Rio de Oro to form Spanish Sahara. Morocco and Mauritania have been in joint control since Spain left the area in November 1975, and the name changed to Western Sahara. After Mauritania withdrew the province Rio de Oro was annexed by *Morocco* and has been renamed Oued Eddahab.

WESTERN SAMOA: full name is *Samoa i Sisifo*; former name is *Navigators Islands*. The islands were awarded to Germany in 1899 but New Zealand seized them in 1914 and gained the League of Nations mandate over them in 1921. The islands were given to New Zealand by the UN as a trusteeship in 1946 and independence was proclaimed on 1 January 1962. Composed of *Savaii*, *Upolu*, Apolima, Manono and some uninhabited islands. *Tokelau Islands* are under Western Samoan administration.

WEST FALKLAND (Islands): alternative name is *Malvina del Este*, part of the *Falkland Islands*.

WEST INDIES: composed of: *Bahamas, Greater Antilles, Lesser Antilles, Barbados, Leeward Islands, Windward Islands*.

WEST IRIAN (Islands): comprising the western half of the island of *New Guinea* and surrounding islands; alternative names are *Irian Barat* and *Irian Jaya*, former names are *Dutch New Guinea* and *West New Guinea*. Composed of Schouten Islands, *Japen Islands*, *Raja Ampat Islands* and Salawati. Part of Indonesia.

WEST MALAYSIA: alternative name for *Peninsular Malaysia*, part of *Malaysia*.

WEST NEW GUINEA (Islands): former name of *West Irian* islands, part of *Indonesia*.

WEST PAKISTAN: former name of *Pakistan*.

WEST SPITSBERGEN (Island): alternative name is *Vestspitsbergen*, part of *Svalbard*.

WEST TIMOR (Island): together with *East Timor* is now called *Timor*. One of the *Lesser Sunda Islands*, part of *Indonesia*.

WEST VIRGINIA: part of *Virginia* until the Civil War, West Virginia then emerged as a separate state and was in 1863 the 35th to join the confederation of the *USA*.

WETAR (Island): one of the *Moluccas Group*, part of *Indonesia*.

WHALSAY (Island): one of the *Shetland Islands*, in *Scotland*, part of the *UK*.

WHIDBEY (Island): part of *USA*, (Washington).

WIGHT (ISLE OF): part of *UK*.

WINDWARD ISLANDS: composed of *Martinique, Dominica, Saint Lucia, Saint Vincent, Grenada*, Saint George and the Grenadines.

WISCONSIN: Wisconsin was acquired by the British in 1763 after the French and Indian Wars and they continued to hold it under pressure after the American Revolution. From 1814 the *USA* took control, transferring Wisconsin from Illinois Territory to Michigan Territory in 1818. In 1836 it emerged as a separate territory and in 1848 became the 30th state to join the confederation of the USA.

WOODLARK (Island): alternative name is *Murua*, part of *Papua New Guinea*.

WRANGEL (Island): alternative name is *Vrangelya*, part of *USSR*.

WYOMING: the Wyoming region was acquired by the *USA* from its European claimants in the Louisiana Purchase (1803) and subsequent annexations. In 1868 the Territory of Wyoming was created, and when it achieved statehood in 1890 it became the 44th member state to join the Union.

Y

YAMDENA (Island): former name is *Jamdena*, one of the *Tanimbar* Islands in the *Moluccas Group*, part of *Indonesia*.

YANBYE (Island): alternative name of *Ramree* island, part of *Burma*.

YAP (Island): one of the *Caroline Islands*, part of the *Pacific Islands (USA)*.

YELL (Island): one of the *Shetland Islands*, in *Scotland*, part of the *UK*.

YEMEN: former names are *South Arabia, Aden Protectorate*, Southern Yemen and *Hadhramaut*. A British crown colony was established at Aden in 1935, the surrounding region became the Aden Protectorate in 1937. The name South Arabia was in use from 1963 to 1967. Independence was gained on 30 November 1967 when the full name became People's Republic of Southern Yemen. The full present name since 1970 has been *People's Democratic Republic of Yemen* or *Jumhouriyat al-Yemen al-Dimuqratiyah al-Sha'abiah*. During the period 1967 to the present the name *South Yemen* has remained in common use. Islands controlled by Yemen are: *Socotra, Kamaran, Perim*, and Al Ikhwan (formerly the Brothers).

YEMEN ARAB REPUBLIC: full name is *Al-jumhouriya al-Arabia al-Yamania*; former name is *North Yemen*. In 1934 Yemen's boundaries were fixed by Saudi Arabia and Britain. Yemen joined the *United Arab Republic* from 1958 to 1961.

YEZO (Island): or *Ezo*, former name of *Hokkaido*, part of *Japan*.

YOUTH (Isle of): former name is (Isle of) *Pines*, part of *Cuba*.

YSABEL (Island): alternative name for *Santa Isabel*, part of the *Solomon Islands*.

YUGOSLAVIA: alternative name is *Jugoslavia*; full names are *Socijalisticka Federativna Republika Jugoslavije* and *Socialist Federal Republic of Yugoslavia*. Yugoslavia came into existence after World War I. It was formally proclaimed in December 1918 as the Kingdom of the Serbs, Croats and Slovenes. A dictatorship was proclaimed in 1929 and the name changed to Yugoslavia. A federal republic was proclaimed in November 1945, comprising the six constituent republics of *Bosnia and Hercegovina, Croatia, Macedonia, Montenegro Slovenia* and *Serbia*. Islands included are: *Pag, Krk, Korcula, Cres, Brac* and *Hvar*.

YUKON TERRITORY: one of the twelve constituent provinces of *Canada*, it was taken over from the Hudson's Bay Company as part of the *Northwest Territories* in 1870. It became a separate territory in 1898.

Z

ZACYNTHUS (Island): alternative name of *Zante*, one of the *Ionian Islands*, part of *Greece*.

ZAIRE: full name is *République du Zaïre*; former names are *Congo Free State, Belgian Congo, Democratic Republic of the Congo, Congo-Kinshasa* and *Kongo*. The Portuguese established ties with the Kongo in the 16th century. In the late 19th century the Belgians unified the area and in 1885 the Congo Free State was proclaimed. Belgium took full control of the area on 28 November 1908 when it became known as the Belgian Congo. Full independence was gained on 30 June 1960 and the name changed to Democratic Republic of the Congo, or Congo-Kinshasa. Soon after this *Katanga* province (now *Shaba*) ceded from the area, but the secession ended on 14 January 1963. The state was renamed the Republic of Zaïre on 27 October 1971.

ZAKINTHOS (Island): alternative name for *Zante*, one of the *Ionian Islands*, part of *Greece*.

ZAMBIA: former name is *Northern Rhodesia*. Livingstone visited Zambia in 1851 and in 1890 Rhodes' British South Africa Company signed protectorate agreements with regional leaders in 1888. In 1911 it became known as Northern Rhodesia. Northern Rhodesia joined the *Federation of Rhodesia and Nyasaland* from 1953 until 1963. Independence was proclaimed on 24 October 1964 when the name changed to the *Republic of Zambia*.

ZANTE (Island): alternative name is *Zacynthus*, or *Zakinthos*, one of the *Ionian Islands*, part of *Greece*.

ZANZIBAR (Island): alternative name is *Unguja*, part of *Tanzania*.

ZEALAND (Island): alternative name is *Sjaelland*, part of *Denmark*.

ZEBU (Island): former name of *Cebu*, part of the *Philippines*.

ZEMLYA ALEKSANDRY (Island): part of *USSR*, (Franz Josef Land).

ZEMLYA GEORGA (Island): part of *USSR*, (Franz Josef Land).

ZETLAND: alternative name for *Shetland Islands*, in *Scotland*, part of the *UK*.

ZHONGGUO: China in Pinyin; see *China*.

ZIMBABWE: former names are *Southern Rhodesia, Rhodesia* and for a short time Zimbabwe-Rhodesia. A protectorate agreement was made between Rhodes' British South Africa Company and the Matabele in 1889. In 1911 it became known as Southern Rhodesia. The *Federation of Rhodesia and Nyasaland* was formed in 1953 and lasted until 1963.

Prime Minister Ian Smith proclaimed a unilateral declaration of independence on 11 November 1965 and a republic in March 1970. The area had become known as Rhodesia in 1964 when Northern Rhodesia proclaimed independence. The area was known as Zimbabwe-Rhodesia after elections in 1979. Further elections in 1980 led to independence on 18 April 1980 and the name was changed to Zimbabwe.